Book of Edward
Christian Mythology

Volume I

Matters Of The Heart

Why will some Christians actually go to Hell? If you are a Christian, this book may save your eternal soul and the eternal souls of your family. Who is Jesus talking about when he said: "I never knew you" in Matthew 7:21-23? Christians! So, which Christians have broken the covenant of Jesus' blood on the cross? Why are they headed to Hell instead of Heaven? The answers are inside.

The Apostle Edward

Introduction

Book of Edward
Christian Mythology

Copyright © 2005 by Edward G. Palmer
Published by JVED Publishing
Elk River, Minnesota 55330

    ISBN 0-9768833-0-9 (Volume I: Matters Of The Heart)
    ISBN 0-9768833-4-1 (4 Volume Set)

Palmer, Edward G.
    1. Faith—The Apostle Edward   2. Bible Prophecy—Christian Mythology
    3. Christianity—Christology

Printed in the United States of America.

All rights reserved. No portion of this book may be reproduced in any form without the written permission of the Author.

Notice. This book and its entire contents represents the sole opinion of Edward G. Palmer based upon his twenty-five plus years of in-depth Bible studies, his actual life experiences, his personal diaries and readily available public records. No part of this book is intended to offer professional counseling of any type especially that of legal advice. Persons involved in cultic churches, those in need of spiritual counseling, medical, legal or any other advice should seek competent professional help.

Capitalization Protocol. On all Bible citations, regardless of the translation used, and where the context clearly points to God Almighty or to Jesus Christ, this book makes the distinction between the two by using either small cap characters or lower case characters. For God Almighty, a small capitalized style protocol is followed and reflected in the format: CREATOR, FATHER, GIVER, HE, HIS, HIM, HIMSELF, YOU, YOUR, ME, MINE, MOST HIGH, MY, MYSELF, LORD and SAVIOR, ETC. For Jesus Christ, a lower case protocol is used except for Lord and Son. Hence, when these pronouns are used for Jesus, they show up as: he, his, him, himself, you, your, me, my, myself, savior, Lord, or Son. This has generally been followed throughout the book, but is not the case with every cited verse. It is used for those verses in which the context cannot be easily disputed or in the case of citing a quality or attribute, which belongs solely to God. For those interested in the original translation capitalization, the author refers them to the actual Bible version used for the cited text. A list of Bible translations is shown on the next page. In some other cases, capital letters used within the cited sentence structure were also changed on common words for ease of reading or modern grammar. In other cases, the capitalized letters were left as shown in the original translation. Hence the original Bible phrase "; Because" might appear as "; because." In all instances, Apostle Edward maintains complete integrity of translation and the writings herein can be traced back to the original Bibles to confirm the accuracy of presentation. While not perfect, the capitalization protocol is fairly consistent and enhances the reading and value of Apostle Edward's teachings.

Introduction

Translation Notice

The following Bible translations were researched for this book along with three Hebrew texts and one or more ancient manuscripts such as the Book of Enoch (ENO). Except where otherwise indicated and in regards to capitalization of words, all Scripture quotations are taken from the Holy Bible, New King James Version © 1979, 1980, 1982 by Thomas Nelson, Inc., Publishers. Verses that are followed by a two, three or four-letter capitalized identifier are from the following Bible translations or reference works.

Abbreviation	Bible Definition
KJV; NKJV	King James Bible[1]; New King James Bible[2]
AMP	Amplified Bible[3]
ASB; NASB	American Standard[4]; New American Standard Bible[5]
DB	Darby Bible[6]
ENO	Book of Enoch — Richard Laurence 1883 Edition[7]
GN; GNB	Good News[8]; Good News Apocrypha[9]-Today's English Bible
GW	God's Word Bible[10]
HEB	Hebrew Bible — English Translation JPS 1917 Edition[11]
JSB	Jewish Study Bible[12] - Jewish Publication Society 1985, 1999
LIV; NLT	Living Bible[13]; New Living Translation[14]
MB	MicroBible[15]
MLT	Morris Literal Translation[16]
MOF	James Moffatt Translation, Final Edition[17]
NIV	New International Bible[18]
NCV	New Century Bible[19]
NJB	New Jerusalem Bible[20]
REB	Revised English Bible[21]
RSV; NRSV	Revised Standard Bible[22]; New Revised Standard Bible[23]
SET	Simple English Translation[24]
TAN	Tanach - The Stone Edition 1996[25]
TB	Transliterated Bible[26]
WEB	Webster's Bible[27]
WEY	Weymouth's NT[28]
YLT	Young's Literal Translation[29]

Copyright 2005 Edward G. Palmer, All Rights Reserved.

Introduction

Table of Contents

Page

Dedication vi

Foreword viii

Prophecies Fulfilled x

Volume I
Matters Of The Heart

Chapter 1: It Starts With The Heart 1

Chapter 2: God Speaks To The Heart... 11

Chapter 3: Repentance From The Heart 28

Chapter 4: God's Call Of The Heart 59

Chapter 5: Practice From The Heart... 72

Chapter 6: The Heart Of An Apostle 93

Chapter 7: Choices From The Heart 131

Volume II
God Does Not Change

Chapter 8: Understanding God's Word 171

Chapter 9: Rationalization of Mankind 204

Chapter 10: The False Trinity Doctrine 242

Chapter 11: God's Eternal Character 312

Chapter 12: The False Salvation Doctrine... 382

Chapter 13: A Light On My Path 416

Chapter 14: The Gift of Jesus 452

Introduction

Volume III
Itching Christian Ears

Chapter 15: Myth — God Heals Everyone 492

Chapter 16: Myth — God Owns Solid Rock 545

Chapter 17: Myth — Giving 10% Is A Tithe 615

Chapter 18: Myth — Abortion Doesn't Matter 678

Chapter 19: Myth — Sexuality Doesn't Matter............................... 749

Chapter 20: Myth — Politics Doesn't Matter 897

Chapter 21: Myth — Everybody Gets To Go 977

Epilogue... 1039

Volume IV
Appendixes—Reference

Appendix A: A Real Salvation Prayer 1043

Appendix B: Baptism Doctrine 1046

Appendix C: Doctrinal Statement 1049

Appendix D: Jackie's Final Thoughts 1069

Appendix E: Ed's Goodbye Eulogy 1072

Appendix F: Cancer Killing Protocols 1083

Appendix G: Illustrations, Tables & Lists 1092

Appendix H: Notes & Bibliography.. 1099

Appendix I: Bible Verse Cross Reference 1134

Appendix J: Index 1177

Copyright 2005 Edward G. Palmer, All Rights Reserved.

Introduction

Dedication

This book is dedicated to my beloved wife Jacqueline Lee (Bowers) Palmer whose love I was privileged to have on this earth for the thirty-nine years of our marriage and the four years of our teen love that preceded it from 1960-1964. On June 3, 2003, God gave Jackie her heavenly wings. This book was started during our thirty-seventh year of marriage and finished in what would have been our fortieth year.

In the forty-three years of earthly love that we shared, God used Jackie to teach me the simplicity of a genuine faith and the resulting earthly righteousness, which is manifested by that faith. Christian mythology has distorted the righteousness message of Jesus Christ. This book sets the record straight again about what it really means to accept God's Son.

———————

Introduction

God also used Dean H. Mattila, Jacqueline Mattila and Vernon Enstad to teach me. They are the three righteous people whom God chose for me, from within the church, to share the spiritual journey of this book with. These three alone had the courage to stand tall for the truth and stand by my side when we left a fellowship of Christians who long ago decided to turn their back on the truth and embrace mythology.

Then there is Michael and Maureen Gill, two righteous people whom God brought into my life uncommitted to Christ at the time and used by God to illustrate as HE did to Peter in Acts 10:34-35 NIV that, "How true it is that God does not show favoritism but accepts men from every nation who fear HIM and do what is right."

Jesus confirms the kingdom requirement of righteousness in Matthew 25:46 with his words: "Then they will go away to eternal punishment, but the righteous to eternal life." In Luke 5:32, Jesus further clarifies this by saying: "I have not come to call the righteous, but sinners to repentance."

This book is also dedicated to the memory of my first son Glen; to daughter Paula & husband James Kantorowicz; daughter Patty & husband Jon Morin; son Brian & wife Brandee Palmer; grandchildren Christopher, Paul, Kathryn, Bradley, Benjamin, Luke, Braiden, Bronson, those yet to arrive and to the memory of grandson Dylan.

This book is also dedicated to the memory of my parents and sister Barbara and all others whom have passed on, to my younger brother James Stanley, his wife Denise and sons Jimmy, John and Nick. This book is also dedicated to Karen and Amy whom God brought into my heart and who will always be like a daughter and granddaughter to me.

Finally, this book is dedicated to the Christian family that my wife and I were raised in. How wonderful to have lived life in a fellowship of people not afraid to talk about the Holy Bible, our God and what it means to have a genuine faith. To those in the family who have wondered why I chose to accept God's calling, the answers will be found in this book. I will always be grateful for all of these special people who shared in my life and I trust that our LORD will find them excellent members of HIS kingdom, even while on this earth and in this present existence. The Apostle Edward

Book of Edward—Foreword

Introduction

Foreword

It was a strange scene for me as I found myself watching television on a recent Sunday morning. As I prepared to leave to open the doors of my own church, I found myself instead surfing with the remote for a few moments. TV is not a high priority for me, but I was interested in seeing what was on the tube in the way of church services. Perhaps for my dear wife who would be taking care of grandkids at home that morning? Perhaps for my grandkids? Perhaps simply for some good content for my own church teachings? It didn't matter.

All of a sudden, I found myself watching the worship service of a church I had heard much about. It was an Assembly of God church in the Minneapolis metro area. The name is not important. What was important to me at the time was what I saw. I was watching a praise and worship service on television and it captivated my spirit. The church was reported by some to be "hot." You know, filled with the Holy Ghost and with signs and wonders. The service was "spirit-filled." I can tell you this by just watching as the people were giving their hearts to God in song, dance, praise and worship.

For years, it was wonderful for me to go up to the altar area, lift my head and arms as high as I could, and praise the LORD. I would sing and dance around the altar getting "drunk" in the Holy Spirit [see Acts 2:15-21]. The object of praise and worship for me was to press into God's Spirit and presence. We are taught in the Bible that through Christ Jesus, we are given the Spirit of truth. We are also taught that it is our ticket to step into the Holy of Holies to be with God.

For me, the worship service was very captivating to watch. I felt myself desiring to "sing, dance, praise and worship" God among those worshippers I saw. The "praise and worship" looked genuine and as my spirit was drawn in further, I sensed my heart crying out: "Make room for me!" There is simply something wonderful worshipping God. We are taught in the Bible that "In HIS presence" is fullness of joy. For me, that is exactly what "praise and worship" is all about—getting into company with HIM. I have never known the level of joy I feel with God in anything of this worldly existence. That isn't to say the world cannot provide you and I with joy. It can, but that kind of joy is short lived. With God, it is always there, it's eternal in nature: you just have to "press-in" to HIM.

Copyright 2005 Edward G. Palmer, All Rights Reserved.

Introduction

As much as I wanted to join the praise and worship service, I couldn't help but wonder: "Who in the crowd was worshipping God in vain?" Who in this particular crowd was going through the motions but inside were not "lovers of the truth?" Who in this particular crowd was still going to Hell yet thinking they were saved? The truth has been perverted from many pulpits and Paul's prophecy in 2 Timothy 4:3-4 was now fulfilled.

You see I recently left a church with this same type of "inviting" praise and worship service. However, Solid Rock Church turned out to be a den of thieves, filled with wicked and unrighteous people [Luke 19:46]. People who consider themselves Christian; yet, who routinely and without much thought ignore the truth. Turning their backs, God saw the fullness of their false witness.

God reminded me of HIS word in Matthew 15:8-9 "These people draw near to ME with their mouth, and honor ME with their lips, but their heart is far from ME, and in vain they worship ME, teaching as doctrines the commandments of men." And again it is written in Mark 7:7 that "They worship ME in vain."

Do you worship God in vain? Many, who call themselves Christians, and who think of them selves as being saved by the blood of Jesus, are simply deluding themselves on the way to their eternal home in Hell. Jesus tells us of this fact. Why? Does it have to be this way?

The message I received from God is to tell those who call themselves Christians that many of them will be going to Hell and that Jesus will serve up a very rude announcement to them as they plead for their eternal soul. However, by that time, it will be too late. So, who are these Christians?

Who is Jesus speaking to in Matthew 7:22-23? Jesus says: "Many will say to me in that day, 'Lord, Lord, have we not prophesied in your name, cast out demons in your name, and done many wonders in your name?' And then I will declare to them, I never knew you; depart from me, you who practice lawlessness." Jesus' message is clearly to those who call themselves Christian. To those who say: "I am saved by the blood of Lamb" or "I know Jesus." This book is a warning to Christians. Many of you are headed to Hell. Why?

The Apostle Edward

Copyright 2005 Edward G. Palmer, All Rights Reserved.

Book of Edward—Foreword

Introduction

Mythology Prophecy

"For the time will come when men will not put up with sound doctrine. Instead, to suit their own desires, they will gather around them a great number of teachers to say what their itching ears want to hear. They will turn their ears away from the truth and turn aside to myths."

2 Timothy 4:3-4 NIV

Truth Prophecy

"The coming of the lawless one will be in accordance with the work of Satan displayed in all kinds of counterfeit miracles, signs and wonders, and in every sort of evil that deceives those who are perishing. They perish because they refused to love the truth and so be saved. For this reason God sends them a powerful delusion so that they will believe the lie and so that all will be condemned who have not believed the truth but have delighted in wickedness."

2 Thessalonians 2:9-12 NIV

Prophecies Are Fulfilled

"The prophecies in 2 Timothy 4:3-4 and 2 Thessalonians 2:9-12 are fulfilled. Today, mythology is routinely taught from the pulpits of many Christian churches instead of God's Holy Word and many people attending Christian churches have turned away from the truth. These people are headed toward Hell unaware of their lost souls."

The Apostle Edward

Matters Of The Heart

Volume I

Chapter One
It Starts With The Heart

"Jesus said to him, you shall love the Lord your God with all your heart, with all your soul, and with all your mind."
Matthew 22:37

"And you will seek Me and find Me, when you search for Me with all your heart." Jeremiah 29:13

"Then I will give them a heart to know Me, that I am the Lord; and they shall be My people, and I will be their God, for they shall return to Me with their whole heart." Jeremiah 24:7

"These people draw near to Me with their mouth, and honor Me with their lips, but their heart is far from Me."
Matthew 15:8

It Starts With The Heart

It starts with the heart. If yours is not 100% committed to God, you will not find Him. It is that simple. For me, this was not an evolutionary process of ever increasing levels of commitment of my heart to God as He challenged me constantly throughout my life to move closer and closer to Him. That is the stuff of Christian mythology. Yes, we know that our faith "comes by hearing, and hearing by the word of God" [Romans 10:17]. We also know that our faith can grow [2 Thessalonians 1:3]. But does our heart fit this type of growth profile according to God's Word? I don't think so.

Your heart is either committed to God or it is not. God did not have a portion of my heart starting at some point in time, which I then increasingly gave more of it as time progressed. No, I was simply not with God growing in faith. My faith started to grow when I became committed to God. At the very point I gave my heart to Him. Before this time, everything was simply only knowledge in my head. It is true; God had been tugging on me. Yet, I was simply not listening to Him and He did not have my heart.

It was an instantaneous decision for me at a time of an epiphany. I will talk more about this in the following chapters. Had a pastor properly trained me in the matters of seeking and finding God, it might have come earlier for me. Yet, I cannot be sure of this, I can only speculate. How do you find God? Have you really found Him? Do you know Him? What He likes? Dislikes? What about you? Does God know you? Has your whole heart been given to Him? Do you hold your ground for righteousness' sake? Would you die on the cross hanging upside down rather than forsake your God? If not, why?

If you don't have the answers to these questions, you can find them in this book. That is a bold statement to make; but, as you read on, you will find out that this is a bold book. It is anointed, ordained and designed by God to awaken His people (Christians, Jews, Muslims and all who sincerely fear Him and who work righteousness) before it is too late. As will be explained later, many Christians will actually be going to Hell and many non-Christians will actually be going to Heaven. You say: "How could this be since to get into Heaven requires Jesus?" What about righteousness?

It Starts With The Heart

What About Righteousness?

"Then Peter opened his mouth and said: In truth I perceive that God shows no partiality. But in every nation whoever fears HIM and works righteousness is accepted by HIM."
Acts 10:34-35

While this book is God's message specifically aimed at Christians, people of all faiths will benefit from God's message in this book. The message originates in the words of Jesus. In Matthew, Jesus tells some Christians: "I never knew you!"

"Not everyone who says to me, 'Lord, Lord,' shall enter the kingdom of Heaven, but he who does the will of my FATHER in Heaven. Many will say to me in that day, 'Lord, Lord, have we not prophesied in your name, cast out demons in your name, and done many wonders in your name?' And then I will declare to them, 'I never knew you; depart from me, you who practice lawlessness!'" Matthew 7:21-23

Exactly whom is Jesus referring to? It is Christians. How do we know that? It is simple, by the words spoken in protest at Jesus' eternal judgment.

"Have we not prophesied in your name *Jesus*?"
"Have we not cast out demons in your name *Jesus*?"
"Have we not done many wonders in your name *Jesus*?"

Ask yourself this question. Would a non-believer be doing these types of things? I.E. Would a non-believer (non-Christian) lay hands on the sick and say: "In the name of Jesus be healed?" Now think about these questions. Does it not require a very bold Christian to prophesy? Does it not require a very bold Christian to cast out demons? How about doing many wonders? I was a Christian for almost twenty years before I got bold enough to lay hands on the sick for healing. The simple facts from Jesus' words are that we are not talking about some newborn Christians.

It Starts With The Heart

It is a fact, Jesus is talking about Christian leaders and others in the hierarchy of the Church who have the courage to boldly speak out and use the name of Jesus. If, what they protest is true, it certainly sounds like some good works to me. Doesn't it? So, what gives? Why would Jesus reject these Christians into the kingdom of Heaven with his astonishing words?

> **Jesus said: "I never knew you!" Matthew 7:23**

At least in this biblical issue, we do not have to guess or languish about any issues concerning biblical interpretation (hermeneutics). Jesus gives us the exact reason when he states: "depart from me, you who practice lawlessness!" That's right, Christians who *practice lawlessness*! What is he talking about? Didn't these people profess Jesus as their Lord? Yes, they did. Didn't they go about the business of good works? Well, it certainly would appear so. Sounds like some kind of works thing to me. And what's up with this? Isn't it true that all I have to do is claim the name of Jesus? Do you mean to tell me that I have to actually do something for my salvation?

This book will provide complete answers to these important questions. It will use as an example of unrighteousness the theft of Solid Rock Church in Elk River, Minnesota. Please note the city and state and don't get this particular church confused with the many others who have chosen such a worthy name for their own. The last time I searched the Internet, there were many churches with this same name: perhaps hundreds around the world. You might have heard: "We are not the tail, we are the head." A reference from this and other Christian pulpits to being "front line warriors for God." As you read on, we will explore some "front-line" issues involved when such a church practices lawlessness and even steals God's property. In the process, we will examine the issue of righteousness and why it is more important to you than the ability to mouth the words "Jesus is my Lord."

Jesus gives us all a clue on righteousness in Matthew 5:20. It is a minimum righteousness standard that is a requirement to get into Heaven. Is there more to getting into Heaven than mouthing, "Jesus is my Lord?" Yes!

It Starts With The Heart

A Minimum Righteousness Standard!

"For I say to you, that unless your righteousness exceeds the righteousness of the scribes and Pharisees, you will by no means enter the kingdom of Heaven." Matthew 5:20

At this point, it would be good to define precisely whom we are talking about when the term Christian is used. Christians are those people who claim salvation through the blood of God's only begotten Son — Jesus. This usually involves accepting Jesus as God's Son who was "raised from the dead" and then confessing this fact with your mouth and believing it with your heart. Here is the biblical process as outlined and explained by the Apostle Paul in Romans 10:8-10.

"But what does it say? 'The word is near you, in your mouth and in your heart' (that is, the word of faith which we preach): [v9] that if you confess with your mouth the Lord Jesus and believe in your heart that God has raised him from the dead, you will be saved. [v10] For with the heart one believes unto righteousness, and with the mouth confession is made unto salvation."

Anything less than this complete *two-step process* [formula] means that you are not really saved by the blood of Jesus. It is confessing coupled with believing. The part left out by most people who call themselves a Christian is: "For with the heart one believes unto righteousness..." Put another way, your belief in God is so strong that you will stand your ground for righteousness. It means you will stand for truth even in the face of severe persecution. Does this describe Christianity today? No, Christians are often the first to turn their backs on the truth. Why?

Yes, I know the Word: "Whoever calls on his name shall be saved." See Acts 2:21 and Romans 10:13. Then take notice that the second reference is located directly at the end of the two-step process. Take heed.

It Starts With The Heart

If you think that being able to mouth the words "Jesus is my savior" means that you are actually saved by Jesus and have assurance of eternal life after you die, think again. This is simply one of the many Christian myths that are now perpetrated in the church during these last days when apostasy rains rampant. However, it is written in the book of James —

"You believe that there is one God. You do well. Even the demons believe and tremble!" James 2:19

The matter of salvation can certainly get confusing. Especially within a church that does not speak the truth and the whole truth of God's Holy Word. For a long time, 1 Corinthians 12:3 seemed to confuse me on this very subject.

"Therefore I make known to you that no one speaking by the Spirit of God calls Jesus accursed, and no one can say that Jesus is Lord except by the Holy Spirit." 1 Cor. 12:3

A particular individual close to my heart could mouth the words that Jesus is Lord. Yet, I often wondered about their salvation because of their behavior. Reflecting back on my own walk with God, I can tell you that at Confirmation in a Lutheran church in 1959 I uttered, "Jesus is my Lord." I can also tell you that in the US Navy in 1963, I signed the Gideon statement in the New Testament to this effect. But I tell you that it wasn't until May of 1978 that I gave God my heart. Prior to this time, and for the first 32 years of my life, it was all head knowledge. I could mouth the words like everyone else. Very easily too. Yet, there is no doubt in my mind that I was not saved until the belief moved from my head and down into my heart.

Ask your pastor "Who is a Christian?" and you might get a multitude of answers. At least one pastor I knew refused to answer the question directly and instead said to me: "Many people believe they are Christian if they get together and worship on Sunday morning." If this sounds like your belief in what a Christian is, it is time to wake up before you face the Judge.

It Starts With The Heart

The best definition I have ever heard of a Christian is a person who has developed a personal relationship with God as a result of accepting and knowing HIS only human begotten Son Jesus Christ. It is the person who has been led back to God by Jesus.

It is God the FATHER who I call my Friend and worship. It is the FATHER whom I ask of and pray to in Jesus' name. It is HIS Son Jesus who I call my brother and friend. It is through Jesus that I can step into the Holy of Holies to worship and fellowship with the FATHER at any time of day or night. It is through Jesus that the FATHER pours out upon me HIS Holy Spirit abundantly, which Jesus refers to as the Spirit of truth. It is God's Holy Spirit that gives me the strength to stand on truth and righteousness. And it is through Jesus, that the FATHER brings HIS kingdom back down to earth for me in this present earthly life. Yes, even in the face of earthly trials and obstacles the FATHER has me living in Eden with HIM in perfect unity, peace and joy. Is this the God you know? Is it the relationship you have developed with HIM?

With the gift of HIS precious Son Jesus, God asks us to demonstrate to HIM that we are responsible people and that we truly have HIM in our hearts. Think about this for a moment. Suppose a friend of yours gives you a brand new Cadillac or other luxury car of your choice. If you are poor, you might be surprised when the gift is complete and comes with a lifetime supply of everything you need (insurance, gas, oil, repairs, maintenance & operational items) absolutely free. All you have to do is enjoy the gift. Right? No!

With such a magnificent gift, you now have responsibilities. A wise man once taught me to watch out for assets, you have to take care of them. In this case, you have to take care of the new car. You drive it, park it, shine it, vacuum it, etc. You keep it in first class shape, don't you? Isn't this your part of the deal? How would your friend feel if he came by later only to find junk all over the seats (you let the kids eat in the car and never clean up after them)? Plus a whole lot of other ugly things like a banged up right front fender you refused to get repaired because you had other more important things to do (like watch television). Maybe you even refuse to get the oil changed because you don't want the bother of taking the time. Even though all these things were provided free to you, it didn't really matter. You simply took things for granted, turned your back on the giver and decided just to run the car into the ground. So, how do you think your friend will feel about it? Pretty bad. Think he will continue to give you gifts?

Well, that is exactly how God feels about all those people who call themselves a Christian and who keep on willfully sinning. God didn't provide you with salvation through His Son free without any responsibility on your part. He expects to fill you with His Holy Spirit and dwell with you back in Eden (on earth in the here and now to accomplish His Will). Just like it was in the beginning with Adam & Eve. Still, maybe you've brought into the Christian myth that all your sins were forgiven forever with the blood of Jesus and now you've got it all in the bank (salvation for eternity).

Let me tell you the truth about Jesus. God's gift of His Son is more about a return to fellowship than about giving you salvation. Salvation is already provided for the righteous and we'll talk more about this later. For now, let's go to the book of Hebrews chapter 10. If you think you have a right to sin after claiming Jesus as your savior, it is only an indication that you may be one of those Christians Jesus is talking about in Matthew 7. You have been taught and have bought Christian mythology. In Hebrews:

> **"For if we sin willfully after we have received the knowledge of the truth, there no longer remains a sacrifice for sins, but a certain fearful expectation of judgment, and fiery indignation which will devour the adversaries. Anyone who has rejected Moses' law dies without mercy on the testimony of two or three witnesses."**

> **"Of how much worse punishment, do you suppose, will he be thought worthy who has trampled the Son of God underfoot, counted the blood of the covenant by which he was sanctified a common thing, and insulted the Spirit of grace? For we know Him who said, 'Vengeance is Mine, I will repay,' says the Lord. And again, 'The Lord will judge His people.' It is a fearful thing to fall into the hands of the living God." Hebrews 10:26-31**

It Starts With The Heart

What? I can't sin? Well, what we are taught is that we cannot continue to willfully sin. There is a difference between willfully sinning and falling short. Sometimes we wind up sinning and we don't have a clue as to how we got there. Jesus will fill the gap in your righteousness. He's just not a replacement for a lifestyle of wickedness (doing things abhorrent to God).

Yes, Christians can lose their salvation through a willful lifestyle of sin abhorrent to God. A lifestyle that treats the "blood of Jesus as a common thing." A lifestyle that insults God. A lifestyle that crucifies Christ again on the cross. How do you know you are on track as a Christian? Start checking yourself to see how often and why you stand your ground on the truth. Turn your back lately on a friend who needed your testimony of the truth? Fail to tell the truth because you didn't want to get involved? If so, brother or sister — you are indeed in trouble with God.

Remember those who really have Jesus have given their hearts to God and HE has given them HIS Spirit of truth. If the truth is not in you, your business, the church or the situation, then God is not a part of it. If you have to pray about doing the right thing (practicing righteousness), God is not a serious part of your life.

Still, many Christians are under the erroneous idea that they should let God take care of it. Let Go & Let God is a popular idea. Don't tell the truth, it only complicates matters and spreads the misery. Let God take care of it. This is the spiritual thing to do? When confronted with evil, God commands and demands that you take a stand for truth and righteousness. Even if you suffer. More about this later. Suffice to say that many people who call themselves Christians are in trouble with God. Perhaps as many as 50% of all who call themselves Christians are really headed for Hell. More on the words of Jesus and his astonishing 50% factor later. So, if you call yourself a Christian, where do you stand in regards to truth and righteousness?

Righteous People Belong To God!

If you are not a Christian, are you a righteous person? If so, you are already in God's hands even if you don't realize it. The righteous are God's!

> "For the eyes of the LORD are on the righteous, and HIS ears are open to their prayers; but the face of the LORD is against those who do evil." 1 Peter 3:12

People who call themselves Christians split 50/50 in recent elections.[1] Half of them voted for the Democratic Party that currently supports abortion, a ban on prayer in schools, homosexuality and a whole list of other things that God finds offensive.

It is estimated that 90% of all black voters voted for this party. Is the Bible really silent on the political and religious issues of our day? Do they really matter to God? If so, why? The biblical answers may shock and even surprise a lot of Christians.

A counselor once asked my teenaged son. "So, on a scale of 1-10, where is God in your life at this time." Not fully understanding the question, the counselor said: "Is God just fire insurance for you or is HE really a serious part of your everyday life?" Before my son spoke, I already knew what his answer would be. I am happy to say that his answer as an adult would be quite different today. What would your answer be?

If God is just fire insurance for you, it may surprise you to learn that your fire insurance policy may have expired. In fact, it may be time for you and your family to re-examine your fire insurance policy (Jesus). It is a simple fact that your actions or lack of actions will betray your heart to the eternal God of salvation. The FATHER has some minimum requirements of us in spite of what you've been taught. That is why John the Baptist taught in Matthew 3:8 that you need to bear fruits worthy of repentance. That is why Jesus taught in Matthew 7:16 that you will know people by their fruits. Put another way, exactly what is your fruit basket filled with these days?

"You Will Know Them By Their Fruits!"
"Therefore, Bear Fruits Worthy Of Repentance!"

It Starts With The Heart

Chapter Two
God Speaks To The Heart

"We have seen this day that God speaks with man; yet he lives."
Deuteronomy 5:24

"Come now, and let us reason together, Says the LORD, Though your sins are like scarlet, They shall be as white as snow; Though they are red like crimson, They shall be as wool."
Isaiah 1:18

"But the wisdom that is from above is first of all pure (undefiled); then it is peace loving, courteous (considerate, gentle). [It is willing to] yield to reason, full of compassion and good fruits; it is wholehearted and straight-forward, impartial and unfeigned (free from doubts, wavering, and insincerity)."
James 3:17 AMP

"And he was called the friend of God." James 2:23

"Adulterers and adulteresses! Do you not know that friendship with the world is enmity with God? Whoever therefore wants to be a friend of the world makes himself an enemy of God."
James 4:4

God Speaks To The Heart

In the first chapter, you learned that with God—It starts with the heart. Your heart should be 100% committed to God. This is the point that will take you beyond the mere physical and into the metaphysical realms of the Spirit as God truly dwells with you and then empowers you for a more satisfying earthly life. Of course, many that consider themselves Christian believe that this spiritual or metaphysical power was reserved for the early church leaders and the first twelve apostles. Or, at least that it only existed during the early periods of the church. God's Word teaches us differently.

> **"But you shall receive power when the Holy Spirit has come upon you; and you shall be witnesses to me in Jerusalem, and in all Judea and Samaria, and to the end of the earth."**
> **Acts 1:8**

> **"And these signs will follow those who believe: In my name they will cast out demons; they will speak with new tongues; they will take up serpents; and if they drink anything deadly, it will by no means hurt them; they will lay hands on the sick, and they will recover." Mark 16:17-18**

> **"And they went out and preached everywhere, the Lord working with them and confirming the Word through the accompanying signs." Mark 16:20**

Acts 1:8 and Mark 16:17-18 are the words of Jesus. After the heart is given to God, the power of the LORD will be released into your life. With your whole heart, God will know that you can be trusted to do HIS work. Having surrendered to HIM — it then becomes a desire of your heart to please and worship HIM. Doesn't this make you a slave? No. Doesn't this severely restrict your happiness on earth? No. When I surrendered to God, my life and happiness exploded. No longer constrained by the fences that I built, I was free to explore the possibilities that God laid before me.

God could have manufactured some stupid robots if he wanted slaves. Instead HE gave us each a free will. The freedom to choose HIM first over earthly issues. In other words, God should have the absolute highest priority within our lives as illustrated below.

God Speaks To The Heart

Priorities

FIRST	GOD	PUT GOD FIRST!
SECOND	**Family**	Sub Priorities a. Spouse b. Children c. Relatives
THIRD	**Yourself**	a. Friends b. Job c. Your Skills
FOURTH	**Church**	a. Friends b. Members c. Committees d. Ushering e. Money $

    Too often being in church is equated with and is treated as if it were on a par or level equal to that of level one. However, this is God's priority level. It is reserved as a place for your heart to reside and commune with God. Some pastors even place the church ahead of God through their man-made traditions and their indoctrination of people. For example: In Matthew 15:1-2, the scribes and Pharisees ask of Jesus: "Why do your disciples transgress the tradition of the elders?" In other words, *your* disciples are not doing it the way we (us elders) say it is suppose to be done (in our church). Put God first and people ahead of material goods and gifts of money to the church in your priorities. Isn't that what Jesus Christ did? Listen to what Jesus said to the scribes and Pharisees in response to their question …

He answered and said to them, "Why do you also transgress the commandment of God because of your tradition? For God commanded, saying, 'Honor your father and your mother'; and, 'He who curses father or mother, let him be put to death.' But you say, 'Whoever says to his father or mother, whatever profit you might have received from me is a gift to God' —then he need not honor his father or mother. Thus you have made the commandment of God of no effect by your tradition." Matthew 15:3-6

It Is Man's Traditions v. God's Commands!

Jesus then teaches the scribes and Pharisees that they have messed up God's commands through their man-made traditions. Here (the church says) it is okay to give all your money to them and then let your mother and father starve or otherwise go in need (because you have no money left in which to honor them according to God's Word). In fact, the church leaders say that by doing this—you honor God. This is the same dogma I have heard in the 21st Century "Word of Faith" church. Nothing has changed in this regard in 2000 years. Should you obey God's commands or the traditions of the elders of your church? The answer should be clear if God speaks to your heart. It must be God's commandments first. They take priority over the church and its doctrines.

For now, what about those priorities shown above? Nobody should seriously argue about whether God should be first in his or her life. If they do, it simply indicates that they are among those whom Jesus is talking about in Matthew 7:22-23 or they are simply NOT meant to be with God. But should your own family be placed ahead of the church in priority? If so, why? God has ordained the church to get the message of "repentance and salvation" out to the world. This is the Gospel of Christ. So, doesn't the church have to take priority over your family? I don't know of any verse that tells you to "take care of the church or you are worse than an infidel" but, the Bible teaches this very message concerning the [your] family.

God Speaks To The Heart

> **"But if any provide not for his own, and specially for those of his own house, he hath denied the faith, and is worse than an infidel [unbeliever]." 1 Timothy 5:8 KJV**

Everyone can now see that God expects you to honor your mother and father and to take care of your family. If you hear anything different from the pulpit of a church, you are certainly attending a modern day Christian cult. What? Christian cults? Yes, they exist and for four years I attended one. It is a fact that some churches are in the God business instead of God's business. Any church that tries to separate you from your family [even if they are all unsaved] in the name of Jesus Christ is a cult. This is not God's way and it is not God's message.

God cares for your entire family and their very salvation may depend upon your fellowship with them. If your church preaches isolation because "you are set aside special for God" — get out of there fast. Suffice to say here that absolutely no compromise should be accepted concerning the basic word of God from any pulpit. Especially so when it comes to fellowship with your family. That includes your brothers, sisters, mother, father, uncles, aunts, cousins, second cousins, third cousins and all other relatives.

Then what about the resources God has for church leaders? Shouldn't these leaders be able to drive around in a BMW, Cadillac, or Mercedes Benz car? Shouldn't they be able to fly from point to point in their own personal Lear Jet with their own pilot? After all, wasn't Jesus Christ this rich? Isn't that the same standard for everyone else "doing God's work?" Jesus gives his own clear instructions to his disciples and they are to travel light. In other words, don't accumulate a lot of assets as you go about God's business.

> **"Go therefore and make disciples of all the nations, baptizing them in the name of the FATHER and of the Son and of the Holy Spirit, teaching them to observe all things that I have commanded you; and lo, I am with you always, even to the end of the age." Matthew 28:19-20**

> "He commanded them to take nothing for the journey except a staff—no bag, no bread, no copper in their money belts — but to wear sandals, and not to put on two tunics. Also he said to them, 'in whatever place you enter a house, stay there till you depart from that place. And whoever will not receive you nor hear you, when you depart from there, shake off the dust under your feet as a testimony against them. Assuredly, I say to you, it will be more tolerable for Sodom and Gomorrah in the Day of Judgment than for that city!' So they went out and preached that people should repent. And they cast out many demons, and anointed with oil many who were sick and healed them." **Mark 6:8-13.**

The message from Christ is clear that these first apostles were to travel light with very few assets. Yet today charismatic church leaders pump out a steady stream of errant teachings concerning the tithe (giving money to the church) in overt attempts to extract every bit of money they can from people for their own dishonest gain. Why? To pay for expensive buildings, planes and cars? For personal luxuries even the very members of their own congregations do not enjoy. Is this your idea of how church leaders should be paid in the 21st century? Do you think this speaks well for the church? After all, weren't all those diamonds meant to be for God's kids? I will give you a clue here and speak more on this later. For now, think about being a friend of the world or a friend of God.

What about those large and expensive churches that men build as they declare their faith to God with ornate dwelling places? Do you think God wants to dwell in those buildings? No. HE wants to dwell inside of you on a one-on-one basis. Those nice buildings are a great place for God's people to gather together. But, the building God wants for HIMSELF is your temple.

> "God, who made the world and everything in it ... does not dwell in temples made with hands." **Acts 17:24**

> "For we are God's fellow workers; you are God's field, you are God's building." **1 Corinthians 3:9**

God Speaks To The Heart

> "Do you not know that you are the temple of God and that the Spirit of God dwells in you?" 1 Corinthians 3:16
>
> "If anyone defiles the temple of God, God will destroy him. For the temple of God is holy, which temple you are."
> 1 Cor 3:17
>
> "For through him we both have access by one Spirit to the FATHER. Now, therefore, you are no longer strangers and foreigners, but fellow citizens with the saints and members of the household of God, having been built on the foundation of the apostles and prophets, Jesus Christ himself being the chief cornerstone, in whom the whole building, being joined together, grows into a holy temple in the Lord, in whom you also are being built together for a dwelling place of God in the Spirit." Ephesians 2:18-22

The temple that God seeks to dwell in is located within your heart. It is not made of man-made materials. About twenty people having this "heart for God" characteristic gathered together at the physical altar of God inside the church's physical building to dance, praise and worship God. As we lifted up our holy hands unto God, we pressed into HIS Holy of Holies for closer fellowship. I was one of those people. As we pressed in closer to HIM, our goal was to simply lose our self. To lose our own identity and to allow HIS Spirit to have its way with us. As our individuality faded, God's glory increased and HIS presence increased. No one can press into God's Spirit like this and stand on his or her own feet for very long. Soon, I was gone. Crashed to the floor like others and totally into HIS presence. I have fallen down on concrete floors and even flew 5-7 feet back from a physical altar to the floor. All without any harm because for me, I was simply letting go of myself and letting God have HIS way with me. I was "pressing in."

The services were awesome and the sheer presence of God Almighty was so very powerful. Many thought it was the music being played; some thought it was the choir singing. Naive pastors think it is their own talents or the power of their own "anointing." I remember one time the volume of singing and the chorus voices I heard was so overwhelming in praise to God

God Speaks To The Heart

that I opened my eyes to see where this beautiful sound was coming from. It was not coming from the musicians and the few singers present. I knew that I had entered into a realm of praise presently shared with the angels of God.

God taught me that HE wants to dwell within the hearts of HIS people. Months later the music changed and the worshippers dispersed to other area churches. Along with the worshippers leaving, God's presence also left. If you do not learn anything else from this book, learn this fact. If you go to a place of worship where people have given their hearts to God, you will find God's presence in that place. For it is found among and within the praise and worship of HIS people. It is not found in a church building. A church that is dead is only that way because it has no heart inside of it for God.

> **"But THOU art holy, O THOU that inhabitest the praises of [your people] Israel." Psalm 22:3 KJV**

God Inhabits The Praises Of HIS People!

> **"But you are a chosen generation, a royal priesthood, a holy nation, HIS own special people, that you may proclaim the praises of HIM who called you out of darkness into HIS marvelous light." 1 Peter 2:9**

Indeed, the temple in which you will find God speaking to you is the temple of your heart. A fully dedicated gift of your heart to HIM winds up getting you back something that is so marvelous that it is indescribable. In HIS presence you will find perfect joy and perfect peace. That is for starters.

> **"We heard him say, 'I will destroy this temple made with hands, and within three days I will build another made without hands.'" Mark 14:58**

What exactly does the word of God have to say about tithing and is your pastor telling you the truth about this aspect of God's Holy Word? The modern day tithe theology is examined later. God's Word may surprise many Christians who have bought into to this area of Christian mythology.

God Speaks To The Heart

You should know that 98% of the Bible could easily be understood simply by reading the words. That is to say, 98% of the Bible is exoteric in nature and is truly meant by God to be understood by all. I.E. God didn't call them the Ten Suggestions, HE called them the Ten Commandments and all of them speak clearly and unambiguously. All we have to do is open up our hearts and let God speak to it. Only 2% or less is esoteric and meant to be understood by only a few (apostles, etc.). To illustrate how God speaks to the heart, examine the Ten Commandments.

Ten Commandments! — Deuteronomy 5:7-21

[1] V7—"You shall have no other gods before ME."

[2] V8—"You shall not make for yourself a carved image any likeness of anything that is in Heaven above, or that is in the earth beneath, or that is in the water under the earth; V9 you shall not bow down to them nor serve them. For I, the LORD your God, am a jealous God, visiting the iniquity of the fathers upon the children to the third and fourth generations of those who hate ME, V10 but showing mercy to thousands, to those who love ME and keep MY commandments."

[3] V11—"You shall not take the name of the LORD your God in vain, for the LORD will not hold him guiltless who takes HIS name in vain."

[4] V12—"Observe the Sabbath day, to keep it holy, as the LORD your God commanded you. V13 Six days you shall labor and do all your work, V14 but the seventh day is the Sabbath of the LORD your God. In it you shall do no work: you, nor your son, nor your daughter, nor your male servant, nor your female servant, nor your ox, nor your donkey, nor any of your cattle, nor your stranger who is within your gates, that your male servant and your female servant may rest as well as you. V15 And remember that you were a slave in the land of Egypt, and the LORD your God brought you out from there by a mighty hand and by an outstretched arm; therefore the LORD your God commanded you to keep the Sabbath day."

Copyright 2005 Edward G. Palmer, All Rights Reserved.

God Speaks To The Heart

[5] V16—"Honor your father and your mother, as the LORD your God has commanded you, that your days may be long, and that it may be well with you in the land which the LORD your God is giving you."

[6] V17—"You shall not murder."

[7] V18—"You shall not commit adultery."

[8] V19—"You shall not steal."

[9] V20—"You shall not bear false witness against your neighbor."

[10] V21—"You shall not covet your neighbor's wife; and you shall not desire your neighbor's house, his field, his male servant, his female servant, his ox, his donkey, or anything that is your neighbor's." Deut. 5:7-21

If you are under the impression that the Bible is hard to understand, please explain to me which part of the Ten Commandments that you do not understand. God is clear enough in these words. The question is: "Where is your heart?" If your heart is with God, the words of the Bible will speak to you with an internal and full understanding. Here is how it works.

Assume you are one of those Christians who think the Bible is a very nice book. You like eternal salvation (fire insurance) but don't think the rest of the Bible is relevant to your life. That is why when you read in verse 19 "You shall not steal" — you don't think it applies to the tools you steal at work or the extra lunch hours you take or even the expense statements you pad. In this case, God's Word does not speak to your heart and you are clearly one of the Christians Jesus is referring to in Matthew 7:22-23.

Now assume that you read verse 19 and you do everything in your power NOT TO STEAL. God's Word is speaking to your heart. If the Dairy Queen cashier gave you change for a twenty-dollar bill when you only gave him a ten-dollar bill, you promptly return the difference. For you, honesty and integrity are actually a part of your life. You do not say to yourself: "That is not my mistake, tough luck." Even if you drive off and are five

God Speaks To The Heart

miles down the road when you realize you were over changed on your order, the next time you are in the store, you refund the extra change (monies).

Too many Christians think that it is okay with God for them to ignore these little areas of theft (sin) in their life. What is at stake here is your own righteousness in God's eyes. As you take care of the little things when it comes to sin, God will give you greater things to handle for HIM. And, in the process, your integrity will increase. Eventually, when you "practice" doing the right thing long enough, it will become second nature. It will become God's nature within you. This is the Spirit of truth in action. God is speaking to your heart and making its desire to stay on course with HIM. There is no such thing as a small or large theft with God. A theft is a theft and you need to understand within your heart that this is God's only reality.

In addition to the priority of your family, God also has concerns about how to communicate with HIM. You can see from Isaiah 1:18 that God has an open door policy of communications. HE says to "come and let us reason together." Godly wisdom is further defined in James 3:17 as also having the ability to be reasoned with. So let's state this very clear here. You have the ability to go and reason with God at any time. HE fully expects all of HIS people to exhibit the ability to be reasoned with. If you cannot reason with your pastor or you are getting a "power play" from him or her, it is time to exit stage right. You are not in God's House! Otherwise you could reason with them. God doesn't simply expect us to shut down our brains and turn them in at the church door. On the contrary, HE expects us to use them.

Then there is the hierarchy of the church. You know, FIRST you need to speak to this person; SECOND, you need to speak to that person. It could take you a long time to get to God if you listened to a lot of church leaders. Some leaders might expect you to travel an obstacle course of people and time (where it takes you 30 days to see the pastor, etc.). The object is to wear you down so you will just forget the issue. A common tactic in the realm of cults. Do you need to see the parish administrator, associate priest, priest, bishop, cardinal and pope before you get to talk with God? If so, it might be time to leave the church you are attending. No one stands between you and God. And, if you need a Mediator, Jesus will help.

God Speaks To The Heart

"For there is one God and one Mediator between God and men, the Man Christ Jesus." 1 Timothy 2:5

There is simply no one between you and God as far as communicating with HIM no matter what you may have heard from various church leaders. God expects to fellowship with you directly. Direct fellowship with the FATHER is a big benefit of Jesus that is totally ignored by the church. Why? Use the Bible as your main reference source. Use your network of people to help you understand and clarify God's Word. This includes the leaders, elders and pastors of your church. However, there can be no compromise on the word of God such as the Ten Commandments. This will represent 90% or more of the Bible to you. Therefore, read the Bible and be confident that God will speak directly to your heart when you open it up to HIM.

God's Communication Plan

God   God

▲▼   ▼▲

You ✝ <<->> Jesus The Mediator

It is no doubt that those who don't know HIM feel that HE is only there to spoil the fun. However, those who know HIM understand that HE is the true King of adventure. When I gave God my heart, the fun started to ramp up on earth. The power started to flow and the fellowship, peace and joy became true realities. In this regards there are a couple of extreme points of view in the world of Christianity. There are those who believe that God does imbue believers (HIS people) with extraordinary powers on earth and then there are those who tend to think of the Bible as a book bordering on fiction or of mere philosophy.

I am always amused at those Christians that hold this second point of view of the Bible. They like to embrace the parts of the Bible that speak of

Copyright 2005 Edward G. Palmer, All Rights Reserved.

Book of Edward—Chapter 2

God Speaks To The Heart

eternal salvation after death for those who claim Jesus as their savior. Yet, they seem to be the first to throw out or dismiss the entire rest of the Bible. The parts with instructions about how to live. My amusement concerns this simple intellectual question. If these Christians cannot trust the entire Bible as God's truth, what makes them think that they can trust only the part of the Bible about salvation through Christ Jesus? Now think about that and ponder how intellectually dishonest that particular point of view is.

Hey, if you can't believe it all, then why waste your time? Jump into secular heaven and don't worry about God's eternal salvation. Isn't that your intellectually honest conclusion if you cannot believe all of God's Word?

The reality is that you can trust the Holy Bible as the inspired word of God. You can read it, understand it and apply its teachings to your life. Once you do this, you will really start to live an interesting life. A life of adventure with God at the helm of your spirit. An excellent resource on this very subject is the book: "Seven Reasons Why You Can Trust The Bible" *by Erwin W. Lutzer © 1998 and published by Moody Press in Chicago.*[1] More about why you can trust the Bible later when I discuss the subject of God's eternal character and hermeneutics (the interpretation of Scripture).

Everyone who is engaged in Bible study should think of the Bible as:

B. I. B. L. E.

Basic Instructions Before Leaving Earth!

Understand the simple fact that nothing in the Bible from God is designed to harm you or limit the degree of fun you can have in this earthly existence. Quite the opposite is actually true in the Bible. Read the Bible with the full understanding that God is telling you how to live a more fuller and satisfying life. When HE says DON'T, there is always a reason. When HE says DO, a reason always exists. God does not take the time to explain HIMSELF to HIS children. When the Word speaks to your whole heart, you will come to understand and marvel at God's power and HIS fellowship.

Copyright 2005 Edward G. Palmer, All Rights Reserved.

God Speaks To The Heart

Does the Bible "speak" to you? If it doesn't, it is because you are approaching God's Word with your intellect and not with your heart & spirit. Someone once said that the reason many people do not understand the Bible is that they are reading some other person's mail from God. In other words, they are trying to understand something that they lack total perspective and details about. These are details that God will fill in for you with His Holy Spirit. When you open up your heart, God will open up your understanding. Intellectuals point out inconsistencies in the Bible as a way of discrediting the Bible, Jesus, the Holy Spirit and God. Why? To steer you away from the eternal salvation that awaits those who trust in God.

Recently, I listened to a program on the life of Jesus. Many scholars were quite disturbed by the fact there is a gap in the life of Jesus. We read in the Bible where he is in the temple preaching at the age of 12 and instantly there he is at the age of 30 starting a ministry. What happened during those critical 18 years? Of course, endless speculation then proceeds from the mouths of these biblical scholars. Who taught Jesus? At least some of the discourse is aimed directly at discrediting God's Word. At raising doubt.

A quick reminder is due. This book is not aimed at convincing you to accept Jesus as Lord and savior. This is a message from God to those who already claim to be Christians. It is a wakeup call from God penned through the mind and hands of yet another willing and yielding spirit. The Spirit of God told me at the time I watched that particular show: "What is this all about and what difference does it really make in the big salvation picture?"

It is irrelevant and it doesn't scratch God's big picture. Still, it can make a difference to those doubtful Christians who are constantly mulling over whether or not they should trust and believe in the Bible. However, I will have to leave that matter between God and them. After all, it is God who calls His people to both HIMSELF and to Christ.

"No one can come to me [Jesus] unless the FATHER who sent me draws him." John 6:44

Let's step back a moment and examine the issue of reading someone else's mail. Could this particular thought hold any truth? Well, consider the following writings from the Bible. Are you reading someone else's mail?

Are They Writing Mail To You?

Paul identifies who he is writing to in Romans 1:8

"To all who are in Rome, beloved of God, called to be saints."

Paul identifies who he is writing to in 1 Corinthians 1:2

"To those who are sanctified in Christ Jesus, called to be saints with all who in every place call on the name of Jesus Christ our Lord, both theirs and ours."

Paul identifies who he is writing to in 2 Corinthians 1:1

"To the church of God, which is at Corinth, with all the saints who are in all Achaia."

Paul identifies who he is writing to in Ephesians 1:1

"To the saints who are in Ephesus, and faithful in Christ Jesus."

Paul identifies who he is writing to in Colossians 1:2

"To the saints and faithful brethren in Christ."

Peter identifies who he is writing to in 1 Peter 1:2

"[To the] elect according to the foreknowledge of God the FATHER, in sanctification of the Spirit, for obedience and sprinkling of the blood of Jesus Christ…"

Peter identifies who he is writing to in 2 Peter 1:1

"To those who have obtained like precious faith with us by the righteousness of our God and savior Jesus Christ."

God Speaks To The Heart

John identifies in 2 John 1:1 who he is writing to.

"To the elect lady and her children, whom I love in truth, and not only I, but also all those who have know the truth, because of the truth which abides in us and will be with us forever."

John identifies in 3 John 1:1 who he is writing to.

"To the beloved Gaius, whom I love in the truth."

Jude identifies in Jude 1:1 who he is writing to.

"To those who are called, sanctified by God the FATHER, and preserved in Jesus Christ:"

John identifies who he is writing to in Revelations 1:1.

"The Revelation of Jesus Christ, which God gave him to show HIS servants — to the seven churches which are in Asia."

Check out some of those vivid descriptions. Those called to be saints. Those sanctified. Those faithful in Christ Jesus. To the saints and faithful brethren in Christ. To the elect. To those obedient. To those with like precious faith. To those who know the truth. To those preserved in Jesus Christ. Do you have some of these attributes?

If you don't fit some of those descriptions, you are truly reading someone else's mail. It might make for some good reading. However, to the extent you are lacking some of these attributes, you will have many gaps in your reading and your understanding will be incomplete no matter how much of an intellectual you consider yourself to be. Plus, no matter how much you have been educated in biblical matters.

On the other hand, if you have given your heart to God, HE will speak directly to it through HIS Holy Spirit. Eventually you will graduate in your understanding to a point where there is no apparent contradiction in the Holy Bible. Only a lack of spiritual understanding by people reading someone else's mail from God. You will graduate to 1 John 2:27.

God Speaks To The Heart

> **"But the anointing which you have received from HIM abides in you, and you do not need that anyone teach you; but as the same anointing teaches you concerning all things, and is true, and is not a lie, and just as it has taught you, you will abide in HIM."** 1 John 2:27

If you feel in your heart that you are really a Christian, do you obey the commands in the Bible? If not, consider these words of the Lord Jesus.

> **"But why do you call me 'Lord, Lord,' and do not do the things which I say?"** Luke 6:46

Could it be the reason that you do not fully understand the Bible is that you have never given God your whole heart? It starts with the heart. Once God has that, HE will then speak to you in a way that will astonish you and HE will give you thrills in life that you never thought were humanly possible. Imagine knowing and fellowshipping with an eternal loving and living God. Imagine what it was like back in the days of Eden when God talked freely with Adam and Eve and they talked freely with HIM, as friends talk with one another. Simply imagine that kind of intimacy with God.

This is where God the FATHER wants to take you with HIS Son Jesus. It's back to HIS fellowship through the gift of HIS Son and the subsequent pouring out of God the FATHER's Holy Spirit upon you in all of its abundance. The resulting imparting of the Spirit of truth to you — fills you with perfect joy and peace. It also gives you the strength needed to stand your ground for truth and righteousness as you live your life for God [even in the face of earthly trials and tribulations]. Standing one's ground for truth and righteousness is <u>the</u> hallmark trait of the true and sincere believer.

> **"God does not dwell in temples made with hands."** Acts 17:24
> **It is the temple of your heart that God wants to dwell in!**

If You Open It Up!
God Speaks To The Heart

Chapter Three
Repentance From The Heart

"God is not a man, that He should lie, nor a son of man, that He should repent. Has He said, and will He not do? Or has He spoken, and will He not make it good?" Numbers 23:19

"Therefore I will judge you, O house of Israel, every one according to his ways," says the Lord God. "Repent, and turn from all your transgressions, so that iniquity will not be your ruin." Ezekiel 18:30

John the Baptist came ... saying, "Repent, for the kingdom of Heaven is at hand!" Matthew 3:2

From that time Jesus began to preach and to say, "Repent, for the kingdom of Heaven is at hand." Matthew 4:17

"Then he [Jesus] began to rebuke the cities in which most of his mighty works had been done, because they did not repent."
Matthew 11:20

"I tell y<u>ou</u> ... unless y<u>ou</u> repent y<u>ou</u> will all likewise perish!"
The words of Jesus — Luke 13:3

Repentance From The Heart

___

God has spoken the exact same message of repentance through the prophets, John the Baptist and then, even through Jesus. You can observe from the preceding verses that repentance is a very serious issue with God. When you give God sincere repentance, God will give you total forgiveness. It all starts when you give God your heart. That is when God starts to speak to your heart. The Bible then becomes a living breathing instruction guide for your life (B.I.B.L.E.). It is the place you turn to find out God's character and what His likes and dislikes are. God will acknowledge you because you have acknowledged Him. From this point, your thinking and reality about God will dramatically change. It is then that true repentance will outpour from your heart effortlessly.

> **"So God, who knows the heart, acknowledged them, by giving them the Holy Spirit just as He did to us." Acts 15:8**

Chapter 2 ended with the statement that standing one's ground for truth and righteousness is the hallmark trait of the true and sincere believer. It is a clear way to identify those who really do walk with God. I could also state this in the reverse. If you observe that a "self-identified" believer fails to stand for truth and righteousness, it is the giveaway mark of the insincere believer. This is the person who talks the talk; but does not walk the walk.

They would like to have you believe that God is embodied within their sins, lies, deceptions and other ungodly behaviors. Or, that God is somehow embodied within their "earthly-focused" desires and compromises. They often offer solutions that are designed to circumvent rather than validate the truth. Let me be very clear. God's Holy Spirit is the Spirit of truth and, if truth is not in the person or the situation, then clearly the living eternal God of truth is also not in the person or situation. God knows your heart. He walks with those who walk with Him.

> **"Good is the opposite of evil, life is the opposite of death, and sin is the opposite of devotion to the Lord."**
> **Sirach 33:14 GNB**

> **"Behold, all souls are Mine; the soul of the father as well as the soul of the son is Mine; the soul who sins shall die."**
> **Ezekiel 18:4**

___

Copyright 2005 Edward G. Palmer, All Rights Reserved.

Book of Edward—Chapter 3

Repentance From The Heart

Closely behind and associated with truth and righteousness is another identifying mark: that of humility and true repentance. Repentance means turning away from sin and returning to God. It means we stop sinning. There are no exceptions to this command in terms of the willfulness of your heart. Those who know God are more likely to know themselves and their true place in God's kingdom. Genuine humility is a sign and indication of true repentance. The humble believer then translates repentance into a lifestyle of obedience that glorifies God and is not into glorifying himself or herself.

The evidence of true repentance is available for all to see in the form of actions easily identified as being changed, new, different and or a part of God. These actions are of such a nature that those people who knew you prior to this moment in time will now find that you truly have changed your heart, your ways. That your thinking is very different. That you are not the same person that you used to be prior to your sincere repentance. Your old behavior has passed away and new behavior is now in your life.

The filthier your sins are at that point in your life, the more dramatic will be the changes in your life. People may even question your sanity because your behavior changes are so dramatic. You may even experience a 180-degree turnabout in areas of your life that you have struggled with for years. In a moment of time, God can give you a complete turnabout in your sinful behavior. That is what happens when God enters the temple of your heart. Indeed, it is often the substance of astonishing miracles in your life.

> **"If indeed you have heard him and have been taught by him, as the truth is in Jesus: that you put off, concerning your former conduct, the old man which grows corrupt according to the deceitful lusts, and be renewed in the spirit of your mind, and that you put on the new man which was created according to God, in true righteousness and holiness." Ephesians 4:21-23**

For example, many Jews in authority doubted the Apostle Paul's true conversion and discipleship. Even those from the original twelve disciples. However, Paul responded with different actions that spoke well of his new

Repentance From The Heart

found belief. Paul's sincere visible actions became a living testimony. It is a characteristic of true repentance. It should be a part of your repentance.

Paul's example of true repentance unfolds in the New Testament beginning in Acts 7:58 — "as a young man named Saul."

> **"As for Saul, he made havoc of the church, entering every house, and dragging off men and women, committing them to prison." Acts 8:3**
>
> **"Then he fell to the ground, and heard a voice saying to him, 'Saul, Saul, why are you persecuting me?'" Acts 9:4**
>
> **And he said, "Who are you, Lord?" Then the Lord said, "I am Jesus, whom you are persecuting. It is hard for you to kick against the goads." Acts 9:5**
>
> *Note: The goad was a staff-like instrument used by farmers to poke at the Oxen plowing their fields to get them to move. Often it had a sharp point at the end of it. Jesus' analogy was an indication to Paul of the uselessness of his behavior in God's larger context. It is like "the Oxen kicking at the goads." It doesn't do the Oxen any good and Paul's actions won't help him either. In modern day parlance, it was like Paul beating his head against a wall.*

Paul had always meant to glorify Jehovah and this experience on the road to Damascus fully revealed to him God's Son. As Paul recognized the Shekinah Glory of God, he also was able to fully understand His Son Jesus. For Paul, God had moved His reality from Paul's head down to Paul's heart.

God's Reality Shifted From Paul's Head To His Heart!

> **But the Lord said to him, "Go, for he [Paul] is a chosen vessel of mine to bear my name before Gentiles, kings, and the children of Israel." Acts 9:15**

Repentance From The Heart

> **Then all who heard were amazed, and said, "Is this not he who destroyed those who called on this name in Jerusalem, and has come here for that purpose, so that he might bring them bound to the chief priests?" Acts 9:21**

Clearly there was confusion among those who knew Paul. "Is this not he who destroyed those who called on this name [Jesus] in Jerusalem?" This is like knowing someone you care about who is a drunkard and who has been that way for several years. You leave for a two-week holiday. When you come back, you find to your amazement that your friend is stone sober and has been that way for the last two weeks. It turns out that on the Sunday you left, your friend went to a church service and gave his or her life to God and accepted the salvation of HIS Son Jesus.

No counseling trips, no trips to Alcoholics Anonymous, no family trips to alcoholic support groups. The family's solution never developed in that manner. Instead, in an instant of time, a sheer moment in your friend's heart, your friend's life was forever changed. This is the stuff talked about when we use the word miracle in Christianity. Yet, for God, it is routine stuff when we give our hearts to HIM. Isn't this what Saul experienced on the road to Damascus? Didn't Saul have a change of heart?

> **"But Saul increased all the more in strength, and confounded the Jews who dwelt in Damascus, proving that this Jesus is the Christ." Acts 9:22**

The Apostle Paul is a good example of what true repentance is really all about. Paul is a man who persecuted and sought to put into prison and to destroy the early believers of the church of Jesus Christ. These people were called Christians because they had accepted Jesus Christ as their savior and had repented of their sins unto God. In the process they were led through, they gave God their whole hearts. For them it meant, that through Christ, they would forever change their behavior in this earthly existence. They had a new perspective. One that now included eternal life and for these new believers, there simply was no turning back to any prior human-only type of behaviors. Commitment meant that there were no alternatives for the rest of their life. Why? Simply because they now belonged to God the FATHER.

Copyright 2005 Edward G. Palmer, All Rights Reserved.

Repentance From The Heart

On the road to Damascus, Saul suddenly found himself choosing this same path [Christ] for his life. God gave Saul a moment to remember that would forever change his life. A confrontation with Jesus in which, he then "knew" Jesus as the only begotten Son of God. It was an experience that Saul would never forget; it was the beginning of a new life as Apostle Paul. The message Paul received is the same one of time immemorial. It was God's message of repentance and eternal life; first through the prophets, then John the Baptist and finally through Jesus, God's Son. Consider these words of Ezekiel. Are they so different from the words of Jesus?

"Cast away from you all the transgressions which you have committed, and get yourselves a new heart and a new spirit. For why should you die?" Ezekiel 18:31

"For I have no pleasure in the death of one who dies," says the LORD God. "Therefore turn and live!" Ezekiel 18:32

God's Message Is Simple: Get A New Life In HIM!

Paul's new life would no longer entail persecuting the new believers who were not understood by the established authorities [Scribes, Pharisees and Sadducees]. Jesus had chosen fishermen at the start of the building of his group of disciples. Now Jesus picked scholarly Paul [Saul], a Pharisee and whose father was also a Pharisee. In addition to these matters of the heart, Paul would also be able to argue for God's Son from an intellectual point of view having been schooled as an advocate of Old Testament Law.

If you examine closely the life of Paul, you will find out that he wasn't a Christian one moment and then the next moment a humanist. He wasn't with God one moment [or day] and not with God the next moment [or day]. He didn't decide to show up for Sunday morning church services so he could be a "good" Christian. Then, the rest of the week, feel free to go about some ungodly business [sinful activities].

No, for Paul had given God the FATHER his whole heart through Christ. Then, he was filled with the FATHER's Holy Spirit. Paul was now "fully hot" to do God's will. Paul's perspective on life and eternity had

Repentance From The Heart

changed. Paul knew that he was going to be dead a lot longer than he was going to be alive in this earthy state. What is your perspective in this regard? Do you as a Christian even have one? In the Apocryphal book of Sirach it is written …

> **"If a person lives a hundred years, he has lived an unusually long life, but compared with all eternity, those years are like a drop of water in the ocean, like a single grain of sand. That is why the LORD is so patient with us, why he is so free with his mercy. HE looks at us and knows that we are doomed to die; that is why HE is so willing to forgive us. A person can show compassion to someone he knows, but the LORD shows compassion for all humanity. HE corrects us; HE disciplines us; HE teaches us. Like a shepherd tending sheep, HE brings us back to HIMSELF. HE will have compassion on us if we accept HIS guidance and are eager for HIM to show us where we are wrong."**
> **Sirach 18:9-14 GNB**

A wise man once taught me, that if I were to be a good man, I should remember four things in life: 1) To love the mother of my children; 2) To give my children a home to grow in; 3) To give my children wings; and, 4) To remember that I too am just passing through this earthly existence.

Like the Apostle Paul, I understand that I will be dead a whole lot longer than I will be alive. I too am just passing through this earthly existence. Again, what is your perspective? Are you so focused on this earthly life that you now have no concern for an eternal life with God? Are you cold, lukewarm or hot for God? As a Christian you should be hot for God. Paul got turned on and he certainly was hot for God. Are you?

> **"So then, because you are lukewarm, and neither cold nor hot, I will spew you out of MY mouth." Revelations 4:16**

As Apostle Paul preached [filled with God's Spirit], he came upon a person who sought to turn people away from God's truth and told him the following hot and timely message:

Repentance From The Heart

> **"Then Saul, who also is called Paul, filled with the Holy Spirit, looked intently at him and said, O full of all deceit and all fraud, you son of the devil, you enemy of all righteousness, will you not cease perverting the straight ways of the LORD?" Acts 13:9-10**

That same hot and timely message of Paul should now be offered to the preachers and pastors of the many pulpits across the world that now routinely lead God's people astray. They do this by preaching a false god of forgiveness that gives the erroneous impression that your behavior during the week is of no consequence to you, "As long as you've got Jesus."

The message continues that, "with Jesus you've got it [eternal life] in the bag." This false god also says you need not worry about the killing of babies by abortion, about being a lesbian or a homosexual. God's grace and love are all you need and they've got you covered? No! You wouldn't find Paul preaching this apostasy junk. Paul had given God his heart. He preached the "straight ways of the LORD."

When Paul gave God his heart, God gave Paul the truth. It started with the heart. Then, once God had Paul's, HE spoke to Paul in an intimate fashion that still exists today. Nothing has changed from God's perspective. In the process, the Spirit of truth was imbedded in Paul. Thus Paul could speak the truth without any fear. Paul turned 180 degrees when he repented.

I can almost hear Paul as he was confronted by many irate people who challenged his new found belief in Jesus Christ. How dare you say that you are now changed. We know you Saul. You persecute Christians! Paul's response was soft and went something like this. "Say what you want to about my past. Even I know that I was guilty as you proclaim. However, none of you can deny the deeds that I now do. Yes, I was that Saul that you knew in the past. I did those terrible things. However, I gave God my heart. Now I am filled with God's Holy Spirit and all that you now see is only Paul. God called me as an apostle to tell the gentiles HIS message of repentance and eternal life. It was the message HE spoke to us through Jesus. Would you like to hear about God's only begotten human Son Jesus and the resurrection of the righteous to an eternal life?"

Copyright 2005 Edward G. Palmer, All Rights Reserved.

Book of Edward—Chapter 3

Repentance From The Heart

A Call To Repentance!

"Come to the LORD, and leave your sin behind. Pray sincerely that HE will help you live a better life. Return to the MOST HIGH and turn away from sin. Have an intense hatred for wickedness." Sirach 17:25-26 GNB

David's Prayer Of Confession And Request For Forgiveness Of Sin!

"Have mercy upon me, O God, According to YOUR lovingkindness; according to the multitude of YOUR tender mercies, blot out my transgressions. Wash me thoroughly from my iniquity, and cleanse me from my sin."

"For I acknowledge my transgressions, and my sin is always before me. Against YOU, YOU only, have I sinned, and done this evil in YOUR sight that YOU may be found just when YOU speak, and blameless when YOU judge."

"Behold, I was brought forth in iniquity, and in sin my mother conceived me. Behold, **YOU desire truth in the inward parts**, and in the hidden part YOU will make me to know wisdom."

"Purge me with hyssop, and I shall be clean; wash me, and I shall be whiter than snow. Make me hear joy and gladness that the bones YOU have broken may rejoice. Hide YOUR face from my sins, and blot out all my iniquities."

"Create in me a clean heart, O God, and renew a steadfast spirit within me."

"Do not cast me away from YOUR presence, and do not take YOUR Holy Spirit from me. **Restore to me the joy of YOUR salvation**, and uphold me by YOUR generous Spirit."

"Then I will teach transgressors YOUR ways, and sinners shall be converted to YOU." **Psalm 51:1-13**

Repentance From The Heart

> "Deliver me from the guilt of bloodshed, O God, the God of my salvation, and **my tongue shall sing aloud of YOUR righteousness.**"
>
> "O LORD, open my lips, and **my mouth shall show forth YOUR praise. For YOU do not desire sacrifice**, or else I would give it; YOU do not delight in burnt offering."
>
> **"The sacrifices of God are a broken spirit, a broken and a contrite heart; these, O God, YOU will not despise."**
> **Psalm 51:14-17**

Apostle Paul responded to God's call and he fully understood David's prayer in Psalm 51. It was a message from Paul's own heart to God. It is a message from my very own heart to God. Like David, Paul was a man after God's own heart. So am I. Dear Christian brother, sister or other child of God — Do you have a heart for doing all of God's will?

> **"I have found David ... [Paul & Edward] a man [men] after MY own heart, who will do all MY will." Acts 13:22 [you?]**

> **"The LORD is always aware of what people do; there is no way to hide from HIM." Sirach 17:15 GNB**

The *American Heritage Dictionary* [1] has the following definition of the word **repent**:

> 1. To feel remorse, contrition, or self-reproach. 2. To feel such regret for past conduct as to change one's mind regarding it: *He repented of his ...* 3. To make a change for the better as a result of remorse or regret.

All of these definitions are good. All of them apply to the Apostle Paul. All of them apply to me. How about you? In addition, can you relate to Job when he replied to God with these words of repentance?

> **"Therefore I abhor myself, and repent in dust and ashes!" Job 42:6**

Repentance From The Heart

If you have never experienced this type of regret and contrition for your sins with God, you may likely be one of those Christians that Jesus is talking about in Matthew 7:21-23 when he said: "I never knew you."

For decades the word of God has been perverted from the pulpits of the Christian church. In the process, many of those would call themselves Christians no longer understand what real repentance is all about. This type of repentance comes from within your heart and involves new behavior. The kind of behavior that is more acceptable to God than your sinful behavior.

Real repentance occurs when a person gives him or herself to God and they immediately stop stealing, promiscuity, lesbianism, homosexuality, etc. Name the sin that enslaves you and keeps you out of fellowship with God.

People Who Are Excluded From Heaven ...

Outside Of Heaven	If God Has Your Heart	Bible Reference
Sexually Immoral	You obey God's sex rules	Rev 22:15
Sorcerers	You do not practice sorcery	Rev 22:15
Murderers	You do not murder	Rev 22:15
Idolaters	You worship only God	Rev 22:15
Lovers of Lies	You are a lover of the truth	Rev 22:15
Practitioner of Lies	You practice truth	Rev 22:15
Unrighteous	You practice righteousness	Rom 1:18, 1Cor 6:10
Ungodly	You practice godliness	Rom 1:18
Fornicators	You obey God's sex rules	1Cor 6:9-10
Adulterers	You obey God's sex rules	1Cor 6:9-10
Homosexuals	You obey God's sex rules	1Cor 6:9-10
Sodomites	You obey God's sex rules	1Cor 6:9-10
Thieves	You do not steal	1Cor 6:9-10
Drunkards	You are temperate	1Cor 6:9-10
Revilers	You do not slander	1Cor 6:9-10

Repentance From The Heart

Extortioners	You do not extort	1Cor 6:9-10
Covetous	You do not covet	1Cor 6:9-10

Many Christians are fully convinced that the blood of Jesus now allows them to conduct themselves in anyway they see fit. However, the word of God teaches us otherwise. The above list is not all-inclusive. It is only a starting point for your own Bible search for truth in the area of sin. If the word of God speaks to your heart, you will take heed and repent to God as needed in any of the above areas. Are you a "slave" to sin?

Some Words Of Jesus Concerning Sin!

Jesus answered them, "Most assuredly, I say to you, whoever commits sin is a slave of sin. And a slave does not abide in the house forever, but a son abides forever. Therefore if the Son makes you free, you shall be free indeed." John 8:34-36

What you observe when a sinner takes a 180 degree turn is the power of God entering the heart of the truly repentant. It is God's power in HIS new temple that seeks to clean up people [the temple]. People who might have tried for years to reform their bad habits are suddenly released from them. When God takes the sin away, you won't have withdrawal symptoms. You will be too busy praising and worshipping HIM for such an awesome act of mercy. It started with the heart. God wants to dwell there. And, when HE dwells there, you won't have to worry about the sins in your life. The major sins will disappear fast when you give God your whole heart.

Apostle Paul did turn on a dime 180 degrees about and ceased forever his sinful behavior of destroying early believers. Like Paul, you too can have that kind of heavenly power come into your life. I have seen this very power in action within other people. I have experienced it in my own life.

Those lingering sins are like climbing a set of steps with God. Your goal is to move from where you are up the steps to where God resides. As you climb up the steps closer to God, the junk [sin] keeps falling and falling

Repentance From The Heart

away. The big and serious junk fell off at the beginning when you gave your whole heart to God. As you climb, the smaller sins [from our poor humanly perspective here] and weaknesses shed themselves away from you step by step as you surrender more and more of your will to God. First came the heart, next is the will. With your heart in God's hands, HE has a chance with your will. The more things you surrender to HIM, the faster the climb. HE will accept you where you are at and help you make the climb to a sin free life. With God holding your hand, get ready for a real life adventure.

It starts with the heart. Then through the blood of Jesus, you are immediately perfect in God the FATHER's eyes. Like any son or daughter who desires to please their father, you endeavor for the rest of your life to do those things pleasing to your heavenly FATHER. You study and read the easy to understand word of God to find out what HE likes and dislikes. The Spirit inside of you rebuilds you from a sinful life into an awesome temple of God. This is not some kind of junk science. This is simply how it works with God. It all started with the heart you gave to God.

You wouldn't think that repentance would be a real issue with "real" Christians. However, I have long lost count of the unrepentant people I have met and known that call themselves Christian. Of course, the intellectual response from many "real believers" will be that "those particular people are not real Christians." This is an allusion to the fact that "true believers" are "truly repentant." This is a debate as old as the Bible. Do a Bible study on the word sincere and you will find the words "sincere faith." Even in times of the early church, there were those who did not walk the talk. This book is being written for all of Christianity. If you are one of the "real" Christians, please excuse the sections that do not pertain to you or that you cannot relate to. I will trust that God is guiding your walk with HIM.

The arguments are more complicated than this in Christianity, as the discussion of sincere repentance usually has to involve sin. For example, I was conversing with a friend on a recent afternoon on this very subject. Agreement was quick on the insincere Christian that "really" never knew Jesus. However, the conversation fell apart when it entered the subject of Hebrews 10:26 which deals with the issue of "continuing to willfully sin." Let me refresh your memory on this very important verse.

Repentance From The Heart

> **"For if we [continue to] sin willfully after we have received the knowledge of the truth [Jesus], there no longer remains a sacrifice for [our] sins." Hebrews 10:26**

The stumbling block in our conversation was two fold. First, the idea of actually losing one's salvation seemed to horrify my friend. Second was his statement: "Well, everyone in the church is a sinner!" Translated, I took the comment to mean: "No big deal, we can't do anything about that with Jesus. Can we?" Part of today's pulpit teachings is the erroneous idea that since we are all sinners, sin no longer matters to God. Especially to Jesus. After all, isn't this the object and purpose of the blood of Jesus? Not only that: "Remember grace; this sounds like a 'works' thing to me." Works?

If I ask you: "Is everyone in the church a sinner?" Your answer would certainly be YES. If I asked you whether Jesus forgave all of your sins, you would again answer YES. And at least one false teacher named Keith told me that that forgiveness extended to all sins I have had in the past as well as those sins I could ever commit in the future. Keith and others like to pick out selected verses and then develop a theology around them. Keith liked Romans 6:10 and similar verses that talked about how Jesus died for all sins. All in this particular verse meaning 100% of the sins of 100% of the people born from time immemorial. All sin ... period ... Once for all.

> **"For the death that he died, he died to sin once for all; but the life that he lives, he lives to God." Romans 6:10**

Keith's intellectual argument had two main points. First, Jesus saves us from all our sins. No argument with that point. Second, we are free to sin, as we want to because of this fact. There can be no doubt that this is a very popular theology among Christians around the world. In fact, very nice indeed. We get to do what ever we want on planet earth. Then when we leave, we get eternal life in Heaven by the blood of Jesus. Pretty cool, huh?

Well, I decided to take Keith's theology to its logical conclusion. I wrote Keith who referred to himself as the "teacher." Dear teacher: You have taught Fred that all his sins are now forgiven not only from the past; but, also those sins that will occur in the future. In fact, you have taught Fred that he is free to sin any time he wants to and in any manner he wants

Repentance From The Heart

to because Jesus died once for all sins. All sin ... period ... Once for all. Is this the theology that you have been exposed to? Do you believe it? I continued the discussion with Keith the "teacher" ...

Teacher, Fred has come in for Christian counseling and here is what he would now like to know. You see Fred claims that he is a serial killer and said he killed five people last month. However, Fred does say that he understands your message that all of his sins are forgiven. All sin ... period ... Once for all. Fred says that in his heart he has accepted Jesus. However, Fred now wants some more assurance that your teachings are true. Fred said he plans on killing another six people over the next 30 days and wants to make sure that those sins will also be forgiven.

So teacher, what should I tell him about the sacrifice of Jesus for those upcoming [future] sins? Are Fred's upcoming [planned serial murder] sins truly forgiven as you say they are? Preposterous arguments for "real" Christians you say? Maybe. But isn't that the kind of sick dialogue that permeates Christianity today regarding sin in our lives? Maybe your sin isn't at the extreme end of killing people, but do you think that God now grades our sins on a curve like some college professor grades math scores?

Sin gets us back now in a full circle to the issue of real repentance. Exactly what is repentance and what is it not? Can one truly repent without actually stopping their sin? If so, how is that done? Or, does repentance by its very nature require us to stop sinning? It would appear, in the serial killer example, that repentance would not make any intellectual sense unless God actually intended for us to stop sinning. Would it? Or, do you still believe that Christians are free to sin in anyway and at any time they choose?

Those Christians who feel they can readily sin any time they feel like it certainly have no intellectual integrity. In fact, these people have bought into some errant theology. The argument is specious and holds no weight from a common sense standpoint with anyone participating in an honest intellectual debate. And as previously shown, it holds no weight with God's Word. Well, what about Jesus? Doesn't it hold some weight with Jesus?

More Words Of Jesus On Sin!

Repentance From The Heart

> Afterward Jesus found him in the temple, and said to him, "See, you have been made well. Sin no more, lest a worse thing come upon you." John 5:14

Jesus said: "Neither do I condemn you; go and sin no more." John 8:11

Walking With God

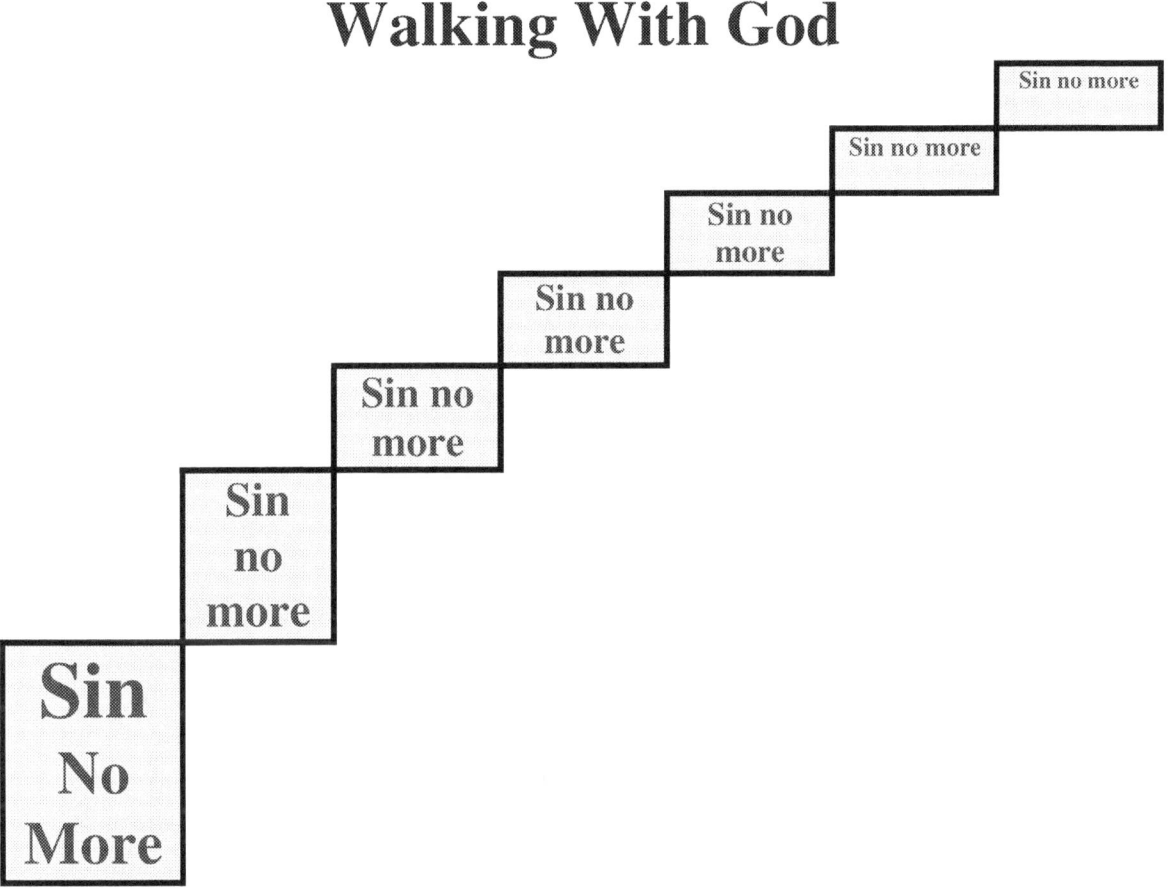

When you really walk with God, all sin is forgiven and all sin starts dropping away from your life. It is like walking up a set of steps toward God the FATHER. The first step is the really big one. That is where you give God your heart. Each successive step you take closer to God finds you more and more pure in your faith and trust. Each step upward you take also finds you with less and less sin. Each step upwards becomes easier and easier as your faith gets stronger and stronger. The sin [gap] you have remaining in your life is covered by the blood of Jesus in as much as it is not willful sin.

Repentance From The Heart

Yes, there is sin that is not willful and even sin that you are not even aware of. God has got those types of sin covered for you with the blood of Jesus. These verses from the Old Testament show clearly that there are other types of sin. There exists sin that is different than that of willful sin.

Unintentional & Unknown Sins!

"If a person sins **unintentionally** against any of the commandments of the LORD in anything which ought not to be done, and does any of them ..." Leviticus 4: 2

"Now if the whole congregation of Israel sins **unintentionally**, and the thing is hidden from the eyes of the assembly, and they have done something against any of the commandments of the LORD in anything which should not be done, and are guilty; when the sin which they have sinned becomes known, then the assembly shall ..." Leviticus 4:13

"If a person sins, and commits any of these things which are forbidden to be done by the commandments of the LORD, **though he does not know it**, yet he is guilty and shall bear his iniquity." Leviticus 5:17

It is clear that, while Jesus forgives all of our sins, Jesus' expectation for all of us is that we would no longer continue to "willfully sin." This is the clear biblical message from God on repentance. A salient characteristic of true repentance is that it is actually followed by a cessation of continued willful sin. That doesn't mean there is zero sin in a person's life.

Now doesn't that salient characteristic of repentance make intellectual and spiritual sense? If you have a changed heart, wouldn't you expect to do things differently in your life? I would. If you find yourself having sinned unintentionally, you still need to repent, as God will hold you accountable. You need to keep a short list of all sins with God. You do this through daily prayer and repentance or by a specific repentance prayer whenever sin sneaks into your life. You will know when sin has crept into your life. God will speak to your heart to set "HIS" will straight with you. As you grow in faith and trust in the FATHER, the Spirit will convict you of sin the moment it happens in your life. HIS Spirit testifies to you concerning real repentance.

> "If we confess our sins, HE is faithful and just to forgive us our sins and to cleanse us from all unrighteousness."
> 1 John 1:9

Apostle John Clarifies The Issue Of Continued Sin!

> "And everyone who has this hope in him purifies himself, just as he is pure. Whoever commits sin also commits lawlessness, and sin is lawlessness. And you know that he was manifested to take away our sins, and in him there is no sin. Whoever abides in him does not sin. Whoever sins has neither seen him nor known him. Little children, let no one deceive you. He who practices righteousness is righteous, just as he is righteous. He who sins is of the devil, for the devil has sinned from the beginning. For this purpose the Son of God was manifested, that he might destroy the works of the devil. Whoever has been born of God does not sin, for HIS seed remains in him; and he cannot sin, because he has been born of God. In this the children of God and the children of the devil are manifest: Whoever does not practice righteousness is not of God, nor is he who does not love his brother." 1 John 3:3-10

Clearly there is a serious issue with God and Jesus concerning the cessation of the willful sin in the life of the believer. If you have not fully grasped this important point as a Christian to date, I hope this chapter has helped to clarify God's Word and how sin and repentance are interrelated. Without sin, there is nothing to repent about. If you call yourself a child of God, then you should be diligent about casting sin out of your life. You should also be diligent about who you associate with. This aspect of the believer's life will be discussed in detail in a later chapter. For now, let God's Word speak to your heart and understand that all sin is evil.

Repentance From The Heart

Let's go back to the dialogue that I had with my friend and the issue of sin within the church. This is another area of great Christian apostasy today. You see, quite frankly, we as Christians are NOT suppose to tolerate sin inside the church. Let's clarify two more specific issues in these regards: a) judging people inside the church; and, b) purging evil from the church. How do these issues relate to our sin and our need for repentance to God?

Paul writes to the church at Corinth that they are to judge those within the church for sin. God's instructions are to purge evil from amongst the congregation and from your fellowship. Really? Sound radical to you? Isn't the church supposed to be a home for sinners? No, actually it is not suppose to be a home to them [willful sinners]. It is suppose to be a home to God's people who have given HIM their hearts and who are intent on worshipping HIM. A lot of confusion is in the Christian church today among believers concerning these issues. The church teaches you to go into evil trenches to claim souls for God. Doesn't it? Then bring souls [evil] into the church?

Note that we are now talking about those who willfully sin and are actually unrepentant with God. Weed them out of the church. They do not belong in the house of God. Those sinners that the FATHER calls into HIS house are already in the process of a radical change of their heart. They are people in the process of giving themselves to God and in need of help or a little guidance. They are already moving toward God and are in repentance. You can see the "progress" they are making in their lives. However, if any in the church are unrepentant sinners, they do not belong in the house of God. Again, you can find these people by the willful sin that continues in their lives. We are told to get the Word out to sinners. We are not told to fellowship with anyone who is a [willful] sinner or with any evil.

Apostle Paul writes about the company we believers should keep.

"I wrote to you in my epistle not to keep company with sexually immoral people. Yet I certainly did not mean with the sexually immoral people of this world, or with the covetous, or extortioners, or idolaters, since then you would need to go out of the world." 1 Corinthians 5:9-10

>>> Judge the morality of those <u>inside</u> the Church! <<<

Repentance From The Heart

> "But now I have written to you not to keep company with anyone named a brother, who is sexually immoral, or covetous, or an idolater, or a reviler, or a drunkard, or an extortioner not even to eat with such a person. For what have I to do with judging those also who are outside? Do you not judge those who are inside? But those who are outside God judges. Therefore put away from yourselves the evil person." 1 Corinthians 5:11-13

>>> God judges the morality of those <u>outside</u> the Church! <<<

The message from Apostle Paul is that we are to judge those people within the Church. Separate yourselves from sinners is the message of the Bible. Judge those who call themselves brothers and sisters. Don't worry about those outside the church, because God judges those outside. Paul writes that you would have to leave the planet if you were to judge all the sinners outside of the church.

Jesus provides a simple process. Confront the sinner first in private. If no repentance occurs, then confront him or her with one or two witnesses. If there is still no repentance, tell it to the church [go public]. Christ says to shun and excommunicate the sinner within the Church who will not repent.

> "Moreover if your brother sins against you, go and tell him his fault between you and him alone. If he hears you, you have gained your brother. But if he will not hear, take with you one or two more, that 'by the mouth of two or three witnesses every word may be established.' And if he refuses to hear them, tell it to the church. But if he refuses even to hear the church, let him be to you [and the entire Church] like a heathen and a tax collector." Matthew 18:15-17

Why should we bother doing this? It gets back to the fruit basket. You will know them [true believers] by their fruits. Therefore, bear fruits worthy of repentance [Matthew 3:8]. How do you know you are keeping company with good or evil people? Examine their fruit. In this case, you examine the behavior of "anyone named a brother [or sister]." Take heed!

Repentance From The Heart

Our obligation to God is to purge out evil from amongst the church. If your church currently tolerates sin and evil like many do, they are not obeying the command of God in this regard. However, when it comes to purging evil from our midst, I have to warn you in advance that we have long since lost and forgot God's perspective on what evil is really all about. That is why some of the following verses may be difficult for you to relate to. Yet, if God speaks to your heart, you will begin to understand evil from God's perspective. After all, isn't that the perspective we are searching for?

Purge Evil From Among You!

"That prophet or dreamer must be put to death, because … he has tried to turn you from the way the LORD your God commanded you to follow. You must **purge the evil from among you**." Deuteronomy 13:5 NIV

"The hands of the witnesses must be the first in putting him to death, and then the hands of all the people. You must **purge the evil from among you**." Deuteronomy 17:7 NIV

"The man who shows contempt for the judge or for the priest who stands ministering there to the LORD your God must be put to death. You must **purge the evil from Israel**." Deuteronomy 17:12

"Then do to him as he intended to do to his brother. You must **purge the evil from among you**." Deuteronomy 19:19 NIV

"If a man has a stubborn and rebellious son who does not obey his father and mother and will not listen to them when they discipline him, his father and mother shall take hold of him and bring him to the elders at the gate of his town. They shall say to the elders, 'This son of ours is stubborn and rebellious. He will not obey us. He is a profligate and a drunkard.' Then all the men of his town shall stone him to death. **You must purge the evil from among you**. All Israel will hear of it and be afraid."
Deuteronomy 21:18-21 NIV

"If, however, the charge is true and no proof of the girl's virginity can be found, she shall be brought to the door of her father's house and there the

Repentance From The Heart

men of her town shall stone her to death. She has done a disgraceful thing in Israel by being promiscuous while still in her father's house. You must **purge the evil from among you**." Deuteronomy 22:20-21 NIV

"If a man is found <u>sleeping with another man's wife</u>, both the man who slept with her and the woman must die. **You must purge the evil from Israel**."
Deuteronomy 22:22 NIV

"If a man happens to meet in a town a <u>virgin pledged to be married</u> and he sleeps with her, you shall take both of them to the gate of that town and stone them to death—the girl because she was in a town and did not scream for help, and the man because he violated another man's wife. **You must purge the evil from among you**." Deuteronomy 22:23-24

"If a man is caught <u>kidnapping</u> one of his brother Israelites and treats him as a slave or sells him, the kidnapper must die. **You must purge the evil from among you**." Deuteronomy 24:7 NIV

"Now surrender those <u>wicked men</u> of Gibeah so that we may put them to death and **purge the evil from Israel**." Judges 20:13

Wow. Unbelievable, isn't it? Imagine, getting purged and having to die for losing one's virginity. Times have changed when you consider that in the early 21st century we now expect our young children to have sex out of marriage. So much so that we pass out condoms to teenagers in some high schools in America. You know what God thinks about that, don't you?

You can surmise from the above ten biblical references quite a few things. First, God expects us to purge evil from among His people. This includes the church of Christ. Second, the definition of evil has been changed by our modern day society. Why, you could get run out of a high school today teaching kids that if they had sex it would be appropriate to stone them to death. And how about that rebellious son? Imagine mom and dad carting the kid off to the edge of town to be stoned to death. Ugh!

God knows something that today's believers have long since forgotten. It is a fact that "People will rise to the level of expectations laid

Repentance From The Heart

before them." I don't think that too many rebellious sons were stoned to death. Nor that too many girls who lost their virginity were stoned to death. Once the word got out after the first one or two, I am sure that there was an "attitude correction" that took place. In modern day parlance, the kids got their "act" straightened out before it was too late. You get the picture here, don't you? God has a very different perspective on sin than most people who call themselves Christians. HIS is a holy and righteous standard.

Now I imagine that the above verses may have really turned off quite a few people that count themselves as Christian. Perhaps even the table on sinners that are excluded from Heaven was a very big turnoff. The questions you have to ask are these: "Is Apostle Edward spewing out his own opinion here? Or, are these words from God verifiable in the Holy Bible as cited? If they are really from the Bible, why should I just ignore them now?"

If I have lost you, I guess you are really just one of the Christians that Jesus is talking about in Matthew 7:21-23. The fact that you've gotten this far is great news for me. It means that you have gotten the main point of the message God has called me to deliver to those "who call themselves a Christian." Congratulations on reading this far. I can see God's stamp of approval coming down. One more job well done for you and Apostle Ed?

Still, there is incredibly powerful stuff coming and I would certainly hate to lose you now over some "purging evil" stuff. Do you really consider yourself a Christian? If so, you had better stick around for the entire ride. Why not let God's Word really open up your eyes. Besides, your eternal life may depend upon it. If you read the whole book, I think God will be talking to your heart before it's over. What a wonderful thing that would be. Now let's conclude this section on evil with some words from Peter.

> **"As obedient children, do not conform to the evil desires you had when you lived in ignorance. But just as HE who called you is holy, so be holy in all you do, for it is written: 'Be holy, because I am holy.' Since you call on a FATHER who judges each man's work impartially, live your lives as strangers here in reverent fear." 1 Peter 1:15-17 NIV**

Repentance From The Heart

Peter's words are important. Live your lives as strangers here [on the earth] in reverent fear [of God]. It is true; you should reverently fear God. Inside your heart, this begins as a healthy respect for God. When HE speaks to your heart, all fear is subdued because of the love you share with HIM. Real believers are "Heaven-focused" and Heaven bound. They know they are just passing through earth on a journey with God — on their way home.

Now that we've moved past purging evil, would you like to know what Jesus' attitudes were concerning those who did and did not repent? There is a wonderful contrast that Jesus supplies us in God's Word.

Warnings From Jesus To Repent Or Perish!

There were present at that season some who told him about the Galileans whose blood Pilate had mingled with their sacrifices. And Jesus answered and said to them, "Do you suppose that these Galileans were worse sinners than all other Galileans, because they suffered such things?" **"I tell you, no; but unless you repent you will all likewise perish."**

"Or those eighteen on whom the tower in Siloam fell and killed them, do you think that they were worse sinners than all other men who dwelt in Jerusalem?" **"I tell you, no; but unless you repent you will all likewise perish." Luke 13:1-5**

He [Jesus] also spoke this parable: "A certain man had a fig tree planted in his vineyard, and **he came seeking fruit on it and found none**.

Then he said to the keeper of his vineyard, 'Look, for three years I have come seeking fruit on this fig tree and find none. Cut it down; why does it use up the ground?' But he answered and said to him, 'Sir, let it alone this year also, until I dig around it and fertilize it.

And if it bears fruit, well. But if not, after that you can cut it down.'" Luke 13:6-9

Repentance From The Heart

In Luke 13:1-5 the message of Jesus is to repent or you will perish. It literally means that you will not have any eternal life. In Luke 13:6-9 the message of Jesus relates to a Christian who has already been planted with "the seed of God" into his or her heart. The wait is on for this believer to bear fruit worthy of his or her eternal life. Fruit worthy of repentance. Jesus indicates that in God's eyes there is a time limit to His patience. Yes, God gets turned off at a certain point in time with those who willfully sin. That is the time when He simply turns His back on you. You might think He is still with you like Samson did when God left him.

> **"And she said, 'The Philistines are upon you, Samson!' So he awoke from his sleep, and said, 'I will go out as before, at other times, and shake myself free!' But he did not know that the LORD had departed from him." Judges 16:20**

There is a point where God will leave you high and dry as the old saying goes. When that is, I have no idea. I only know that God's Word makes it abundantly clear that He will put up with only so much from unrepentant sinners. His forgiveness is awesome, His patience is wonderful and His grace is truly without measure. Still, His Word makes it abundantly clear that there are limits He has with us "mere" humans. Then there is this wonderful contrast from Jesus Christ.

Jesus Contrasts A Sinner Who Repents
"The Sinner Who Repents Brings Joy In Heaven!"

Parable of the Lost Sheep

Then all the tax collectors and the sinners drew near to him to hear him. And the Pharisees and scribes complained, saying, "This Man receives sinners and eats with them." So he spoke this parable to them, saying: "What man of you, having a hundred sheep, if he loses one of them, does not leave the ninety-nine in the wilderness, and go after the one which is lost until he finds it? And when he has found it, he lays it on his shoulders, rejoicing."

Repentance From The Heart

"And when he comes home, he calls together his friends and neighbors, saying to them, 'Rejoice with me, for I have found my sheep which was lost!' "

"I say to you that likewise there will be more joy in Heaven over one sinner who repents than over ninety-nine just persons who need no repentance." Luke 15:1-7

Parable of the Lost Coin

"Or what woman, having ten silver coins, if she loses one coin, does not light a lamp, sweep the house, and search carefully until she finds it? And when she has found it, she calls her friends and neighbors together, saying, 'Rejoice with me, for I have found the piece which I lost!' "

"Likewise, I say to you, there is joy in the presence of the angels of God over one sinner who repents." Luke 15:8-10

Parable of the Lost Son

Luke 15:31-32 sums up this joy and merriment with the words of Jesus in this parable of the lost son.

And he said to him, "Son, you are always with me, and all that I have is yours."

This is a message for the righteous who does not need to repent.

"It was right that we should make merry and be glad, for your brother was dead and is alive again, and was lost and is found."

This is a message for the sinner who is sincere in his or her repentance. Joy is in God's kingdom when your heart repents.

Kingdom Joy Occurs When Sinners Repent!

Repentance From The Heart

Can you see the wonderful contrast Jesus speaks of? When a sinner repents — there is joy in the Heavens. Also note that the righteous already have all that God has to offer. Jesus speaks of this in Luke 15:31. Many Christians think they have a lock on God because we claim the blood of Jesus. However, as we will see from the word of God, there is such a thing as a righteous person who already belongs to God. This is also a topic that might disturb Christians who have come under the false idea that only they will be going to Heaven. However, this is a subject worthy of its own chapter. For now, let's close this one with a final thought on repentance.

Christians are under the impression that they can forgive someone who does not repent. Often, the words of advice go something like this: "You should forgive him, her or them for your own sake. Forgiveness is for you and not for them." Does the dialogue sound familiar? Over the years, we have come to confuse bitterness with forgiveness. It is a biblical fact that you cannot forgive someone whom does not first repent. Forgiveness is not for you; it is for the sinner or person who has trespassed against you. Does God forgive unrepentant sinners? No. Neither can you.

Still, you should not allow any bitterness to come into your life. This is where the phrase "let go and let God" really does have application in your life. When a person sins against you and is unrepentant in the matter, you cannot forgive them. What you can do is to give the matter over to God and move on with your life. Simply refuse to become embittered by the incident involved. Trust God to take care of it. It is God who says: "Vengeance is MINE and I will repay." You could, if you wanted to—simply place the matter into God's hands instead of festering over it and becoming bitter.

One particular verse in the Bible that may account for this kind of theological thought on forgiveness is Isaiah 43:25 which reads:

"I, even I, am HE who blots out your transgressions for MY own sake; and I will not remember your sins." Isaiah 43:25

The King James Version uses the word "blotteth" which occurs only once in the entire Bible. According to Strong's Concordance, the usage of this word is derived from the Hebrew word **machah**, maw-khaw.'

Repentance From The Heart

___

The Hebrew word means to literally rub out or erase — abolish, blot out, destroy, put out, reach unto, utterly, wipe (away, out). God is telling us that HE "blots" out completely our transgressions for HIS own sake. This verse should not be construed as God providing forgiveness when we do not repent because of the very next verse and the entire chapter context.

> **"Put ME in remembrance; let us contend together; state your case, that you may be acquitted." Isaiah 43:26**

The principle of forgetting any transgression against us and "blotting" it out [of our mind] is very important to remember. By choosing to let God handle something that you are not fully equipped to handle, you will feel a great sense of relief. The Bible teaches, "Love covers a lot of sin."

However, the lack of repentance and your desire to simply "forget about the incident" does not excuse you from your duty to God. It does not give you excuse to turn your back on evil. If a crime has been committed, it is your duty to report it to the appropriate authorities before you choose to "forget about the incident." Some Christians choose the path of turning their back on evil because they don't want to get involved. This only perpetuates evil and gives it credibility. A holy God who says: "State your case, that you may be acquitted" will not view turning your back lightly. I hope you can distinguish these subtleties and God's need for us to "purge evil."

Forgiveness is a very serious spiritual issue with God that cannot be ignored by Christians. I suspect it is also not fully appreciated by many Christians. If someone comes to you and repents, you must forgive him, her or them. You do not have an option here if you know your Bible. You must forgive or your FATHER in Heaven "may not forgive you." Indeed, this is a very serious issue worthy of a more detailed discussion later. For now take a look at what Luke 17 says concerning forgiveness.

> **"Take heed to yourselves. If your brother sins against you, rebuke him; and if he repents, forgive him. And if he sins against you seven times in a day, and seven times in a day returns to you, saying, 'I repent,' you shall forgive him."**
> **Luke 17:3-4**

___

Copyright 2005 Edward G. Palmer, All Rights Reserved.

Book of Edward—Chapter 3

Repentance From The Heart

The operative words in the above verse are "if he repents." You have no business forgiving someone who does not repent. To do this only reinforces sin and evil. It also reinforces the bad behavior. You should also know that there are limits on forgiveness. We already discussed the limits of God above and that we could not pin down the exact point in time that HE will turn HIS back on the sinner. Yet, Jesus gives us another lesson that many Christians now take to mean an "unlimited" amount of forgiveness.

> **"Then Peter came to him and said, 'Lord, how often shall my brother sin against me, and I forgive him? Up to seven times?' Jesus said to him, 'I do not say to you, up to seven times, but up to seventy times seven.' " Matthew 18:21-22**

Seventy times seven is four hundred and ninety. Metaphorically, you might take this verse to mean an unlimited amount of forgiveness is due from your heart to anyone who feels that they can trample on it. We'll talk more about hermeneutics [Bible interpretation] later on. However, for now you should understand that the plain word of Jesus does spell out a formula that derives a fixed maximum times to forgive others ($7 \times 70 = 490$ times). In today's world, many people can push you to that high limit very fast. Yet, at some point, isn't the sincerity of the repentance questioned?

You are created in God's image and HE has some limits. So don't think for a moment that this is not a good upper limit to work with from a purely human perspective. You should forgive the way God does. After repentance occurs and only up to the point where you are obviously being taken advantage of. I think that is the point where God turns off. It is interesting to note that in Luke 13 a full three years had passed without any fruit being given and only another year was available for results. This too may be a metaphor, but then again it may be HIS timing. After four years of efforts, you've been given enough time for fruit to surface. God moves on?

It is time to wrap up this chapter and I hope the information provided will lead you into your own serious Bible study on sin and repentance. In some respects I have only scratched the surface on this key subject matter. Before leaving the subject, I want to share with you my own prayers of repentance that I use. Remember to keep a short list of your sins with God.

Repentance From The Heart

Daily Repentance Prayer!

Heavenly FATHER, forgive me for the sins that I have committed in thought, word and deed. Forgive me for the sins contained in my dreams, those sins that I am even unaware of and for every way in which I have fallen short of the goals YOU have for my life. Forgive me FATHER for any way in which I have disappointed or displeased YOU.

FATHER, bless me this day indeed. Enlarge my territory, my ministry, my influence and my finances that I might do thy will more effectively. FATHER, keep your hand on my shoulder and your Spirit in my heart and mind that I may truly know THY will. FATHER keep me from all evil that I may not cause any pain. FATHER, in Jesus' name, I ask these things of you.

Specific Repentance Prayer!

FATHER forgive me for I have sinned* by _____

_____

_____

Spell your sin out in detail above. Don't try to hide anything from God!

The second paragraph in the daily repentance prayer above is based on 1 Chronicle 4:10. This is where you will find the prayer of Jabez. This is a prayer from Jabez' heart and the Bible says that God answered his prayer. It is the type of prayer that gets a response because it comes from the heart. Go to your local Bible bookstore and ask for the small book with the same name [2]. It will deepen your prayer life with your Heavenly FATHER.

The adventure with God started at the point that you gave your heart to HIM. Suddenly you found yourself with a set of new thoughts to go along with a new and changed heart. It was then that God started to speak to you. Through HIS Holy Word and through a soft inner voice that now seems to guide you along the paths of HIS righteousness.

Copyright 2005 Edward G. Palmer, All Rights Reserved.

Book of Edward—Chapter 3

When you gave your heart, it was simply the trigger that set off a series of chain reactions. Your heart now leads you and keeps you on the paths of righteousness and sincere repentance. His Spirit walks with you and helps you walk the talk effortlessly. You work daily to serve a holy God by eliminating sin, evil and wickedness wherever and whenever they confront you. Yours is a new life filled with the Spirit of a holy God.

There are many aspects to the issue of repentance and I sincerely hope you have enjoyed reading this chapter as much as I have enjoyed writing it. For all the hours I spent up late at night has been in the presence of a holy and awesome God. It is He whom I have come to share my life with. It is He that I serve. It is He that I yield my tired body to. It is He that gives me the strength to continue on and it is He that I trust. He is my source of joy, peace and of everything I need in life. This is the loving God that I know and now share with you. If your heart is open to God, your life will begin a new journey with Him as you continue reading this book.

> **"Cry aloud, spare not; lift up your voice like a trumpet; tell My people their transgression, and the house of Jacob their sins." Isaiah 58:1**

"Father, in the name of Jesus, I ask that you open the heart, eyes and minds of all who read this work that you have ordained by my hands. Lord, restore righteousness into the hearts of all who call themselves Christian."

The Apostle Edward

It Started By Giving God Your Heart, Then, God Spoke To Your Heart!

Now Comes Sincere Repentance From The Heart

Chapter Four
God's Call Of The Heart

"But he is a Jew who is one inwardly ... of the heart, in the Spirit, not in the letter; whose praise is not from men but from God." Romans 2:29

"Now the LORD had said to Abram: 'Get out of your country, from your family and from your father's house, to a land that I will show you.' " Genesis 12:1

"Then Jacob made a vow, saying, 'If God will be with me, and keep me in this way that I am going ... so that I come back to my father's house in peace, then the LORD shall be my God.' "
Genesis 28:20-22

"God called to him from the midst of the bush and said, 'Moses, Moses!' And he said, 'Here I am.' " Exodus 3:4

"Then Mary said, 'Behold the maidservant of the LORD! Let it be to me according to your word.' " Luke 1:38

"You, therefore, who teach another, do you not teach yourself? You who preach that a man should not steal, do you steal?"
Romans 2:21

God's Call Of The Heart

Have you ever had that sinking feeling set into your gut accompanied by a sudden and literal fearful expectation of impending judgment? The kind that overwhelms your body as either the Police or Highway Patrol turns on its lights from behind your car? You are being pulled over for some kind of violation. Maybe someone was with you and the very first words out of their mouth were: "Now what did you do?" Next is: "You know the Police do not pull people over for nothing. You must be guilty of something!"

Maybe the action was somewhat more dramatic and unnerving as they also turned on the siren. As if to literally scream at you: "Pull over or else." Else what? That is a good question, but we never get that far in our minds. Our heart is too busy thumping. It seems that all we can do in that moment is to keep looking back through the rear view mirror wondering. Wondering if they really caught you as you were speeding or otherwise disobeying traffic laws. Maybe simply just wondering with shattering nerves exactly what it was all about?

I suspect the Police and Highway Patrol initially just turn the lights on so as not to make such a big deal out of pulling your car over. However, when the siren goes off, that really gets the heart thumping fast. I know, I have been there. Usually speeding. I am better about this now. Still, on a long distance trip, this is something I need to keep working on. I must confess that usually when the heart thumping goes on, at that moment "I am guilty as sin." At the moment I may even be angry with myself — that I got caught. Sound familiar? Maybe you've had an encounter of your own.

The terror we experienced when the Police "pull the car over" is similar to other horrifying experiences we have in life. These would include getting a letter from an unknown law firm; getting served with lawsuit papers [the legal process unfolding against you]; and, appearing before any Judge in any Court for any reason.

If you can't relate to these examples, how about the horror of watching your one year old baby fall down a long flight of steps and hitting the concrete floor in the foyer. That is what happened to my daughter Patty last Saturday.

Copyright 2005 Edward G. Palmer, All Rights Reserved.

God's Call Of The Heart

It was almost like slow motion and there was virtually nothing she could do to intervene. My grandson Luke took a spill on the date of his first birthday party. I saw Patty's red swollen eyes and the fresh tears falling down her face. I witnessed her terror and noticed the horrific thumping of her heart immediately after the event occurred. Of course, one-year old Luke was fine and didn't miss a beat from his busy play activities. Isn't that just like kids? They move on fast from their trials in life; but we adults have to pick up the pieces of our traumatized souls. Luke was fine, but his mom was traumatized. Someone told her: "He's okay: You can put your heart back in your chest now." No doubt that is exactly what she had to do. For in that brief moment of time, Patty's heart started thumping with tremendous anxiety about what had just happened. Along with the fear of what the outcome would be.

As Luke's grandfather, I saw everything immediately after the fact. Luke came out into the garage party area and started to play "as if" virtually nothing had taken place. He was only 12 months old and has been walking since he was 10 months. Consider this: What if I, his grandmother or the both of us had been nearby witnessing the entire event as his mother did and equally being unable to do anything to stop it? Do you think our hearts would have been thumping out of our chests also? You better believe it. Along with anyone else who witnessed the accident but couldn't do anything about it. Sheer terror sets in and it sets in fast during such events. These are only a few of the many fearful experiences we suffer through while in this earthly existence. Our fears extend beyond ourselves and to those we love. Terror comes for our family members and us.

Patty may have remembered the time as a little girl she fell down her grandfather's steps into his basement. A huge set of about 26 steps that had a concrete floor at the bottom. Nobody was there to witness; but, as she was ready to slam into the floor, her grandfather by sheer happenstance walked around the corner from his workshop and she landed safely into his quickly outstretched arms. It was divine fate. Yes, we all just marveled at God's providence that day. And we hated to even think "what if?"

Copyright 2005 Edward G. Palmer, All Rights Reserved.

Book of Edward—Chapter 4

God's Call Of The Heart

The nature of these and other fearful experiences in life is identical to the kind of experience that willful sinners can expect at the hands of God. Only magnify the fear and anxiety about 100-1000 times. Great fear. That is an important message for all Christians. Reading further in Hebrews 10 we find out more of God's Word on this subject of fearful expectation.

A Certain Fearful Expectation Of Judgment!

"For if we sin willfully after we have received the knowledge of the truth [Jesus], there no longer remains a sacrifice for sins." Heb 10:26

"But a certain fearful expectation of judgment, and fiery indignation which will devour the adversaries." Heb 10:27

It is those words "a certain fearful expectation of judgment, and fiery indignation" that captured my attention at 1:45 a.m. this morning. I had just finished writing Chapter 3 and as I left my office, I was very tired. So tired that I just meandered down the highway at a slow pace. I wasn't in a hurry and no one was on the road at close to 2 a.m. It was foggy and my thoughts of the moment were to just take my sweet time driving home.

I hadn't noticed that the local police were now following me. They had seen me pull out of my office in the business section of the highway. It was highly suspicious in their eyes since the local auto dealer next door often gets burglarized during the night. They followed me up the highway to main street about two miles. As I prepared to turn left, I still hadn't noticed that I was being followed. I turned and then within 1/4 block began to turn left over a bridge. My house was less than a mile away; when suddenly, the police turned their lights on. At 2 a.m. their lights lit up the sky and it seemed that they had every kind of strobe light and advanced light beam that was available in the year 2001. At least that is what it seemed like to me.

God's Call Of The Heart

It was a very disturbing event and yet strangely enough I was absolutely calm and without any of the suspected typical "heart throbbing" that one can experience as the Police lights terrorize your soul. When the officer came over to the car, I politely asked what the problem was. He said: "We saw you drive out of the business area and were curious." I quickly explained that I was working late in my office and who I was. I then asked if there was something wrong with my driving to which he responded: "No, your driving was fine. We were just curious." I then proceeded on my way.

As I continued down the road, it dawned on me how calm I felt about the whole situation. You see, I knew inside of my heart that I was totally innocent in the matter and that I had nothing to worry about with the Police. It was the opposite of some prior experiences in which I knew I was "guilty as sin" and my heart thumped and throbbed heavily. I was then "fearful" of what the outcome of the impending judgment would be.

I marveled at the strange inner peace that I had driving the rest of the way home. I hadn't gone far when God reminded me that this was HIS type of inner peace I was experiencing because "I knew" that I was not guilty.

How and where did I know? I just knew in my heart. As a young man I imagine I gave my dear wife Jackie quite a lot of grief. We have been married 37 years now and I have long since quit asking about how it was that "she knew." Of course this is the humorous communication issue that exists between men [especially young men] and women who just happen to think a little different. In my younger left-brain only days, she would make a statement and I would ask: "How do you know?" She would politely say: "I just know." Which, of course, would absolutely drive me nuts. However, women are natural at "just knowing" and they needn't have any reason for it. They are just naturally intuitive, holistic and spiritual in areas that provide answers from within the soul and without reasoned explanation.

Men should learn more about this. I certainly have. Nobody who "just knows" inside of them needs to explain themselves to others. This time "I just knew' that I was not guilty of anything and that I had absolutely nothing to sweat or to even get excited about. God reminded me that the

Copyright 2005 Edward G. Palmer, All Rights Reserved.

Book of Edward—Chapter 4

opposite of the peace that I felt was that fearful expectation I had felt at other times. HE reminded me that it applied to unrepentant willful sinners.

All of the fear that people feel in these types of situations stem from the uncertainty of the outcome of the Judge. Now, if we can feel that bad physically over those in human authority that judge us, how much worse do you think it will be when God judges us — if we are guilty? The writer of Hebrews continues on with further explanation in verses 10:28-31.

> **"Anyone who has rejected Moses' law dies without mercy on the testimony of two or three witnesses."**
>
> **"Of how much worse punishment, do you suppose, will he be thought worthy who has trampled the Son of God underfoot, counted the blood of the covenant by which he was sanctified a common thing, and insulted the Spirit of grace?"**
>
> **"For we know HIM who said, "Vengeance is MINE, I will repay," says the LORD. And again, "The LORD will judge HIS people. It is a fearful thing to fall into the hands of the living God." Hebrews 10:28-31**

"It Is A Fearful Thing To Fall Into The Hands Of The Living God!"

Those who claim salvation through Jesus will be held to account for their actions. If they continue to willfully sin, they have cheapened the gift of God and "counted the blood of the covenant ... a common thing." Now if you have just given someone your most prized possession, wouldn't you be very angry if they didn't take care of it, especially if they had no sense of "duty" to take care of it? Those Christians who continue to willfully sin are in serious trouble with God. "It is indeed a very fearful thing."

Paul says that the "real" Jew is one who has the stuff inside their heart, in the Spirit, not in the letter; whose praise is not from men but from

God's Call Of The Heart

God. Do you worry more about men than you do about God? This would include your boss, your neighbors, your clubs and yes, even the people from your church. Does their human voice carry more weight in your considerations than that of God's Word? It shouldn't. If you call yourself a child of God, make sure your heart concurs and doesn't betray you.

When you give your heart to God, you won't have any trouble packing your bags and heading "west" like Abraham did. Can you imagine the response of your parents as you tell them you are heading west? Where to? Oh, I don't know. Just west. Why? God told me to pack up and head in that direction. Sure? You can imagine the rest of the conversation with the family. I suspect this is what the typical missionary suffers through unless they come from a family dedicated to God and everyone in it can bear witness to the call on the person going on the mission trip. Without a heart for God, people think in human terms and this may color their judgment.

Then there is the Christian whose family isn't supportive for various reasons. Some churches teach them to say "get thee behind me Satan." No one should feed his or her parents that particular line. Right or wrong, God still expects you to honor your mother and father. It is unscriptural to simply dis your folks to have your own way in life thinking it is God's will. It isn't. Honoring your mother and father is the very first promise in the Bible. The promise is that you will live a long life. If your folks don't agree with your choice, don't alienate them in the name of God. It is wrong. Find another way to work with them on the issue. A way that brings honor to your parents. When you honor your parents [even when they are wrong], it is evident that God has your heart.

When you give your heart to God, you won't have any problem calling HIM LORD of your life. That is what Jacob did when he made a vow to God. Jacob was a thief. Yet God was with him when he gave up his heart and Jacob knew it. It was a moment of joy for Jacob. His search in life was over. God was now in control of the situation and life was going to be different, everything was going to be okay from that moment forward. When you acknowledge that God is in control of your own life, God has your heart.

God's Call Of The Heart

When you give your heart to God, you won't have any problem saying: "Here I am" like Moses did when God called from the burning bush. Moses was a murderer having killed an Egyptian. Do you think he was interested in going back to Egypt? Why me, LORD? God explained that HE had chosen Moses for the task. Moses yielded to God's will. It is okay to ask: Why me LORD? I have done this on several occasions. However, when HE gives you the answer that you are chosen, the discussion is over. When you can yield your will to HIS, God has your heart.

The most important question to now ask yourself is: "How do I know that this [name your issue here] is God's will for my life?" How can I really discern God's will for my life? There are four principles that I have come to trust in concerning God's will for my own life. All four of these principles are important in discerning God's will. They are.

1. When God won't leave you alone concerning a particular matter, then you will know it is God who truly speaks to you.

2. When the issue at hand FULLY lines up with God's Holy Word, then you will know it is God who speaks to you.

3. When the issue at hand involves only the truth, then you will know that it is God who speaks to you.

4. When your own heart feels right about the issue and the spirit inside of you confirms to you that it is God's will, then you will know that it is God who speaks to you.

Now let's illustrate two examples. I remember several times when I got a message in which "I just knew" it was God who was talking to me. One of those times, I was shaving and looking in the mirror when the message came to me as follows: "Go and tell the pastor of the church that they need to change the name of the church." I think this was one of those times I looked around to see if someone was speaking to me out loud. Of course, no one was there and I knew it was HE. I remember talking back out loud as I shaved: "Why should I go and tell them? I don't even belong to that church. I am only visiting there." The response was to go do it for ME.

God's Call Of The Heart

However, when you get one of these "I know it is God speaking" events, there is always a small additional thought that maybe your own imagination is getting carried away. So, you just conveniently let it go. You simply say: "That's nice; I think I will forget about it now." That is you do exactly what I suggested you not to do with God. You should not turn your back on HIM concerning any issue. However, the FATHER is an awesome God and HE is not afraid to bring the subject back up for further discussion.

In this case, HE knows you are ignoring HIM but HE persists with the matter anyway. After about 3-4 weeks of getting the same message thrust upon me, I then know for sure that it is from HIM. That is because, as humans, we are good at setting aside issues and forgetting about them. Unless, we are being reminded or nagged about them. It's a little like forgetting to make the bed or take the garbage out. It is hard to forget if mom or dad is there to constantly remind you. After 4 weeks, I finally told the pastor. What a strange experience that one was.

I suppose it is somewhat also like the conversation that God had with Adam and Eve in the Garden of Eden, which went like this:

> **"And they heard the sound of the LORD God walking in the garden in the cool of the day, and Adam and his wife hid themselves from the presence of the LORD God among the trees of the garden. Then the LORD God called to Adam and said to him, 'Where are you?' " Genesis 3:8-9**

Do you believe for one moment that God did not know precisely the location of where Adam and Eve were hiding? Of course HE knew; but that is the kind of heavenly FATHER you have. HE has a certain amount of humor and playfulness in HIS character. HE is certainly willing to dialogue with you and to play the game in order to find out exactly where your heart is in the matter. When the issue won't leave you alone and no one human is bugging you about it, you will know it is God that is talking.

Another illustration comes to mind concerning a particular pastor I knew that was anxious to put someone into the mission field. There was a conflict with a particular family and the parents of the wife. To get his way

God's Call Of The Heart

in the matter the pastor counseled the couple to tell the wife's parents "Get thee behind me Satan." The message from the pastor is that he was <u>anointed</u> of God and knows what is best for the couple in this matter. The fact that the wife's parents didn't agree with the pastor meant that the wife's parents were on Satan's side and wanted to obstruct "the work 'God' had planned."

A red flag should go up here because God has told you to honor your "father and mother" that you may live a long life. God never promised you that your parents would always be right. Does God's Word speak to you?

If the word of God speaks to you, it would be time to tell the pastor that he is sinning against God. The pastor would not preach the word of God and then violate it, would he? Guess again! Some pastors do exactly that. It is not new and has been around since time immemorial. Still, it is shocking to the unsuspecting believer. Especially those who place their trust in a pastor and are ignorant of God's Holy Word on the subject. If you are naïve and uneducated in the Word, a pastor could simply pull a power play and you would be unable to discern the pastor's wickedness. Consider the words of Apostle Paul in Romans to teachers who do not walk the talk.

> **"Indeed you are called a Jew [the teachers of the day], and rest on the law, and make your boast in God, and know HIS will, and approve the things that are excellent, being instructed out of the law, and are confident that you yourself are a guide to the blind, a light to those who are in darkness, an instructor of the foolish, a teacher of babes, having the form of knowledge and truth in the law."**

> **"You, therefore, who teach another, do you not teach yourself? You who preach that a man should not steal, do you steal? You who say, 'Do not commit adultery' do you commit adultery? You who abhor idols, do you rob temples? You who make your boast in the law, do you dishonor God through breaking the law?"**

> **"For 'the name of God is blasphemed among the Gentiles because of you,' as it is written." Romans 2:17-24**

God's Call Of The Heart

As hideous as it may seem, your very own pastor may be leading you astray from God's truth. Especially concerning repentance. Paul writes earlier in the same chapter the following words on *the impenitent heart*.

Impenitent Hard Hearts Treasuring Up Wrath!

"But in accordance with your hardness and your impenitent heart you are treasuring up for yourself wrath in the day of wrath and revelation of the righteous judgment of God, who 'will render to each one according to his deeds' ":

"Eternal life to those who by patient continuance in doing good seek for glory, honor, and immortality; but to those who are self-seeking and do not obey the truth,"

"But obey unrighteousness — indignation and wrath, tribulation and anguish, on every soul of man who does evil, of the Jew first and also of the Greek;"

"But glory, honor, and peace to everyone who works what is good, to the Jew first and also to the Greek. For there is no partiality with God." Romans 2:5-11

If the Bible teachings from your church do not line up with the simple word of God, you might have to leave the church and find a fellowship of believers that stand in HIS truth. However, before you go make sure you inform everyone you know including the pastor on why you are leaving. Would you leave your friends in a den of thieves or a pit of evil? Isn't that exactly what Christians do when they leave a church filled with apostasy because of evil, but fail to counsel those that they know on their knowledge? Don't turn your back on evil. God says to purge evil. If you are in the position to fight for righteousness within your church—that is a better course of action to take. Gather up a grievance committee and take the word of God to the elders, deacons and pastors. If they won't repent, make it public.

Remember, at least 98% of the Bible is "exoteric" and is meant to be understood by all. That includes you too. You can use the four principles I

God's Call Of The Heart

cited above as your guide to knowing God's will. When you can discern God's will for your life and you choose to obey it, God truly has your heart.

When you give your heart to God, you won't have any problem saying: "Let it be according to YOUR Word" like Mary did when she was informed that she was going to be impregnated by the Holy Spirit. You can just imagine the family dynamics of that one. Can't you? Still, do you think it mattered to Mary? No. God had her heart.

Mary's prayer was the same kind as Jabez's prayer in 1 Chronicles 4:10. It was a simple prayer from the heart. It was: Use me LORD. It was: Have your way with me LORD. When you can pray like Mary and Jabez and really mean it, God truly has your heart.

These are some examples of the many people whom God has called and who said yes. They were not perfect people. Many had problems of sin. However, they all decided to give God their heart and start anew with HIM.

For me too, a day came when I suddenly met God. Like others, I had ignored HIS call and wandered in my own wilderness for the first thirty-two years of my life. Like others, God had never stopped calling me even when I wasn't really listening. Then one day "I knew" HIM. I had wandered enough and struggled enough on my own. Much like Jacob and others, I had my own baggage full of sin. It didn't matter with God. HE was patiently waiting for me to exhaust my options. I think that is exactly what happened to me on a spring day in May of 1978 when I finally looked upward and said: "I understand God. From now on you lead and I will follow."

That was the day I stopped trying to live life on my own. That was the day my intellect became insufficient and my spirit started to kick in. Looking back I now recognize all of the flag waving that God had done to get my attention in my early years. How HE orchestrated my life and placed me in position to get the Word eventually. Why did it take me thirty-two years? That is a question I now ask with tears in my eyes. Tears of sadness that so much of my life was not lived to the fullness it could have been had I lived it with HIM. The tears come from a repentant heart knowing the depth of the love that God must have for a sinner like me.

God's Call Of The Heart

How did I get to this point in my life where I would gladly be hung upside down and crucified on a cross before I would betray HIM? How did I get to the point in my life that the depth of HIS love for me would permeate my entire being?

How did I get to the point in my life that I am able to share HIM so freely with others? How did I get to the point in my life when asked: "Don't you do anything on your own anymore? — I can easily answer no, I don't." And when asked: "Do you do everything that God tells you? —I can answer, yes." These are the questions that family and friends will ask of you as they now wonder what is going on in your life. What happened to the Ed that I used to know? Are you a religious zealot now? Not really, I guess I am simply a changed man. I am no longer the person that I used to be. I have shed the old man and have now put on the new man. For it is written ...

"If indeed you have heard him and have been taught by him, as the truth is in Jesus: that you put off, concerning your former conduct, the old man which grows corrupt according to the deceitful lusts, and be renewed in the spirit of your mind, and that you put on the new man which was created according to God, in true righteousness and holiness." Ephesians 4:21-24

"Yes, I Guess I Really Am A Changed Man!"

How did I get to the point where I would dare accept HIS mantle of apostle and dare bring HIS message to you? First, I gave God my heart. Second, I listened to HIM when HE started speaking to my heart. Third, I gave HIM a true repentance from my heart. And, fourth — I chose to accept HIS call upon my heart [life] regardless of the consequences that it may bring to me. If you are reading this book, God may have a call on your life. If so, the question for you is this: "Will you also accept God's call?"

After True Repentance, Comes ...
God's Call Of The Heart

Chapter Five
Practice From The Heart

"I will praise YOU … with my <u>whole heart</u>." Psalm 9:1

"I will praise the LORD with my <u>whole heart</u>, in the assembly of the upright and in the congregation." Psalm 111:1

"Blessed are those who keep HIS testimonies, who seek HIM with the [their] <u>whole heart</u>!" Psalm 119:2

"With my <u>whole heart</u> I have sought YOU; oh, let me not wander from YOUR commandments!" Psalm 119:10

"And yet for all this … Judah has not turned to ME with her <u>whole heart</u>, but in pretense," says the LORD. Jeremiah 3:10

"If we say that we have fellowship with HIM, and walk in darkness, we lie and do not practice the truth." 1 John 1:6

"Whoever does not practice righteousness is not of God."
                                                    1 John 3:10

Practice From The Heart

Apostle Paul Boldly Proclaims: "I Do Not Lie!"

"I am in Christ, and I am telling you the truth; I do not lie. My conscience is ruled by the Holy Spirit, and it tells me I am not lying." Romans 9:1 NCV

Apostle Paul wrote that he "serves God with his whole heart" in Romans 1:9 NCV. The New King James Version reads "whom I serve with my spirit." You can conclude from these two translations that serving God with your "whole heart" is tantamount to serving God with "your spirit."

"But you are not ruled by your sinful selves. You are ruled by the Spirit, if that Spirit of God really lives in you."
Romans 8:9 NCV [Part A]

"But the person who does not have the spirit of Christ does not belong to Christ." Romans 8:9 NCV [Part B]

"If you use your lives to do the wrong things your sinful selves want, you will die spiritually. But if you use the Spirit's help to stop doing the wrong things you do with your body, you will have true life." Romans 8:13 NCV

"The true children of God are those who let God's Spirit lead them." Romans 8:14 NCV

Yes, it is possible to live your life "ruled" by God's Holy Spirit and Apostle Paul tells us how in Romans 8:9 with the operative word "IF." *If that Spirit of God really lives in you*, then your life is ruled by the Spirit. Paul continues on immediately by stating further in verse 9 [Part B]. *If you do not have the spirit of Christ,* then you do not belong to Christ.

Note two points here and the apparent contrast from Paul. **First**, you are ruled by the Spirit of God **IF** the Spirit of God lives in you. **Secondly**, you belong to Christ **IF** you have the spirit of Christ. I will come back to this particular topic later in the book for more of God's Word and further study. For now, reread this section of Romans 8 using the NKJV Bible.

Copyright 2005 Edward G. Palmer, All Rights Reserved.

Book of Edward—Chapter 5

> "So then, those who are in the flesh cannot please God."
>
> "But you are not in the flesh but in the Spirit, if indeed the Spirit of God dwells in you. Now if anyone does not have the spirit of Christ, he is not his."
>
> "And if Christ is in you, the body is dead because of sin, but the Spirit is life because of righteousness." Romans 8:8-10

Is it possible to be led by the Spirit of God [in righteousness] and yet not know Jesus Christ? Maybe, having never even heard about Jesus? Yes. Is it possible to have the spirit of Christ and yet really not know God? No. We will deal more with this area of conflict in Christianity later in the book. Before we get there, do some thinking about the Spirit of God and the spirit of Christ. Are they the same? Different? Is Christ God? Why would Paul use this language? Why didn't he simply state in the second half of verse 9 "If anyone does not have the Spirit of God, he is not His [God's]?" Can some people belong to God and others to God through Christ Jesus His Son?

For the moment, Paul seems to have literally "hit the nail on the head" concerning the controversial topic of "real Christians vs. false Christians" when he used the operative word **IF** in verse 9. Real Christians do have the Spirit of God dwelling within them. The Holy Spirit influences their actions and you can actually "know them by their fruits [actions and the results of their actions]." This explains why Paul can write with passion in Galatians.

> "I have been crucified with Christ; it is no longer I who live, but Christ lives in me; and the life which I now live in the flesh I live by faith in the Son of God, who loved me and gave himself for me." Galatians 3:20

The modern Christian songwriters Phillips, Craig & Dean in their 1996 song Crucified With Christ (Star Song) write: "For I have been crucified with Christ ... and yet I live. Not I ... but Christ who lives within me." Every time I hear their song, it just thrills my soul. I can literally just let this song cycle and cycle and cycle. My heart leaps with joy inside as the Spirit of God testifies to me about the validity of that statement: "I am

Practice From The Heart

crucified with Christ." Are you crucified with Christ? If not, why? Are you really then a Christian? Isn't this also a hallmark sign of the true believer?

Paul at the very depths of his soul simply knew that he could not do God's will on his own. He needed help. The solution was the Spirit of God, which Paul found through his faith in Jesus. Paul had taken a step through a spiritual gateway [Christ] in time back into fellowship with the FATHER. As Paul found himself in the loving caring arms of his heavenly FATHER, he also discovered that he was back in Eden on planet Earth. In the midst of trials and sufferings, Paul found perfect peace and the fullness of joy! These flow only from the FATHER [God].

> "LORD, I know the way of man is not in himself; it is not in man who walks to direct his own steps." Jeremiah 10:23
>
> "YOU will keep him in perfect peace, whose mind is stayed on YOU, because he trusts in YOU." Isaiah 26:3
>
> "YOU will show me the path of life; in YOUR presence is fullness of joy; at YOUR right hand are pleasures forevermore." Psalm 16:11

If you think earthly pleasures are great, then you haven't really tried the pleasures from Heaven that result in "perfect peace"; "fullness of joy"; and "pleasures forevermore." There is simply no comparison. No matter how much money and resources you have acquired on planet earth, it will never bring you this type of peace, joy and pleasure. When you walk with God's Spirit, then you will truly start to live an exciting adventuresome life. Even if you first are crucified in Christ and even if you still have to "suffer."

James tells us to "count it all joy when you fall into various trials." Why? James gives us the answer immediately by stating: "The testing of our faith produces patience." Still, doesn't this sound weird? Joy in the midst of trials? I can tell you from my own walk with God that James is telling the truth. In the midst of your trials, God will be there "inside of you with HIS kingdom." Then you will know what Jesus meant in Luke 17:21.

Copyright 2005 Edward G. Palmer, All Rights Reserved.

Book of Edward—Chapter 5

Practice From The Heart

> **Jesus said: "The kingdom of God isn't ushered in with visible signs. You won't be able to say, 'It has begun here in this place or in that part of the country.' For the kingdom of God is within you." Luke 17:21 Living Bible**

Yes, Jesus said, "the kingdom of God is within you." If you think about this and meditate on this verse, you will have to conclude that it is you and only you that are in the driver's seat concerning the eternal destiny of your soul. Only you can make the choices that will either lead to eternal life or to eternal damnation. Only you can choose to obey God or to ignore HIM. However, no matter how hard you try to ignore HIM, you cannot avoid the eventual emptiness and the feeling that you lack something very important. This is because God's laws are "in your mind and written on your heart."

> **"But this is the covenant that I will make with the house of Israel after those days, says the LORD: I will put MY law in their minds, and write it on their hearts; and I will be their God, and they shall be MY people." Jeremiah 31:33**

> **"For when Gentiles, who do not have the law, by nature do the things in the law, these, although not having the law, are a law to themselves, who show the work of the law written in their hearts, their conscience also bearing witness, and between themselves their thoughts accusing or else excusing them." Romans 2:15**

> **"For this is the covenant that I will make with the house of Israel after those days, says the LORD: I will put MY laws in their minds and write them on their hearts; and I will be their God, and they shall be MY people." Hebrews 8:10**

Clearly God did not create you with the intention that you would have to live this earthly life on your own [spiritually speaking]. As HIS creation, the design was for us to live in daily fellowship with HIM. To live in Eden knowing only the goodness that God and this earthly life had to offer. We are a long way from that perfect picture and we are certainly out of practice.

Practice From The Heart

Back to Apostle Paul. He was very out of practice [fellowship with God] at the time of his conversion on the road to Damascus. Do you then think that God made him perfect once again [on his own]? Or, did Paul now have to get back into practice? Well, how about the Apostle John who wrote the following compelling words on sin? Was Apostle John perfect? Sure sounds like it, doesn't it? He cannot sin! Can you?

> **"Whoever has been born of God does not sin, for HIS [God's] seed remains in him; and he cannot sin, because he has been born of God." 1 John 3:9**

"He Cannot Sin, Because He Has Been Born Of God!"

Paul stated in Romans 9:1 that — "I do not lie." We have previously discussed God's Spirit, as the <u>Spirit of truth</u> and that if the truth is not in the situation then God is not in it. Speaking a lie is sinning and God has some strong words to say about this type of behavior in Revelation chapter 22.

Who Can Enter Heaven?

> **"Blessed are those who do HIS commandments, that they may have the right to the tree of life, and may enter through the gates into the city." Revelations 22:14**

Who <u>Can't</u> Enter Heaven?

> **"But outside are dogs and sorcerers and sexually immoral and murderers and idolaters, and whoever loves and practices a lie." Revelations 22:15**

We have already studied in Hebrews chapter 10, God's Word about willfully sinning after having received Christ. The Bible teaches us that anyone who does willfully sin [at this point] no longer has the blood of Jesus covering his or her sins. In fact, such a person has serious judgment from God awaiting them for treating HIS Son in such a "cheap" and "common" fashion. This has to be the "ultimate insult" to a holy and righteous God.

Practice From The Heart

Clearly you should have learned from God's Word that there are certain expectations that HE has on the part of believers [who are sincere]. The two major questions now looming in this chapter are: Do we have to be perfect? Or, is it — practice, practice, and practice?

Is it possible to be a Christian and yet be a liar? Is it possible to be a Christian and tell even a single lie? A single small lie? A single very small white lie [whatever that is in our modern twenty-first century culture]?

What is God telling us when HIS Word talks about "lying and not practicing the truth" in 1 John 1:6? Exactly what does it mean to "practice" righteousness as we are told to do in 1 John 3:10? Do you suppose the very word "practice" has connotations that speak of some duty and action on the part of Christians? Again we are forced to confront the issue of whether we actually have to do something for our salvation or if it is simply a free ride, as many Christians now believe. What do you think?

Clue: Does the receipt of any valuable free gift <u>ever</u> carry with it any responsibilities on the part of the recipient? If so, under what conditions and why? Or is the recipient of the valuable gift free to do with it as they wish. After all, a gift is a gift, isn't it? Don't confuse the nature of receiving a free and valuable gift with the responsibilities associated with owning it. Also, think about under what conditions your behavior towards the valuable free gift might be construed as either a direct insult or lack of respect towards the giver. By others observing your attitude towards the gift? By the GIVER HIMSELF? Review the discussion on page 7 for more thought on this subject.

For now imagine that you are a Christian in Nazi occupied Holland during World War II and you are hiding Jews in your attic to save them from the death chamber. Maybe you are hiding Anne Frank, her father Otto and their family up there in your secret place. You have hidden the entrance to the attic with a clever bookcase that now conceals the extra space you have. If the Nazi's find these Jews, you know that they plan to kill them.

Suddenly, the door rings and a Nazi officer who is backed up by 15 Nazi soldiers asks you the pointedly direct question: "Are you hiding any Jews in your home?" "JUDANS???" What would your answer be?

Practice From The Heart

You hesitated as you said NO because you realize "in your heart" that you are now lying on top of everything else. Perhaps Revelation 22:15 just flashed across your mind. You want to serve God and you take HIS Word very seriously. You certainly don't want to be considered a "practitioner and lover of lies." Still, you think, this particular situation must be different in God's eyes?

The officer then pulls out his Bible because he knows that you claim to be a Christian. He turns quickly to Romans 13 and reminds you that your Bible commands you to tell the truth and to obey the authorities that now rule over you. Your mind thinks: "Now what should I do?"

If you think this sounds like a far-fetched scenario, think again. It has actually happened and only God knows how many times. Yes, you did lie! You chose to attempt to save the lives of the Jews you were hiding. You reasoned correctly that God would not hold this particular lie against you.

You reached the limits of your human understanding. You only knew that you wanted to do what was right for God's people. In the process, you also found out that you couldn't be "perfect" on your own in this matter.

Jesus Asks: "So, You Want To Be Perfect?"

Parable Of The Rich Young Ruler!

"Now behold, one came and said to him, 'Good teacher, what good thing shall I do that I may have eternal life?' So he said to him, 'Why do you call me good? No one is good but ONE, that is, God. But if you want to enter into life, keep the commandments.' "

"He said to him, 'Which ones?' Jesus said, 'You shall not murder, you shall not commit adultery, you shall not steal, you shall not bear false witness, honor your father and your mother, and, you shall love your neighbor as yourself.' "

Practice From The Heart

> "The young man said to him [Jesus], 'All these things I have kept from my youth. What do I still lack?' Jesus said to him, 'If you want to be perfect, go, sell what you have and give to the poor, and you will have treasure in Heaven; and come, follow me.' "
>
> "But when the young man heard that saying, he went away sorrowful, for he had great possessions."
>
> "Then Jesus said to his disciples, 'Assuredly, I say to you that it is hard for a rich man to enter the kingdom of Heaven.' "
>
> "And again I say to you, it is easier for a camel to go through the eye of a needle than for a rich man to enter the kingdom of God." Matthew 19:16-24

Don't think for one moment that Jesus was saying that this rich young ruler was not going to get into Heaven [have eternal life]. That is not the message of Jesus in this parable. Actually, just the opposite occurred. Jesus confirmed to this rich young ruler that he would get into Heaven by his words in verse 17 when he says: "But if you want to enter into life, keep the commandments."

Keeping God's Commandments Means Eternal Life!

Right about now, many Christians will be faced with a very difficult choice to make. Maybe this is you? Should I believe the church that says I have to do nothing for my eternal life? Or should I listen to the words of Jesus who tells me that eternal life will come to me by keeping God's commandments? Ever hear this message preached from a pulpit?

The choice for you is clear. Choose to listen to God's Holy Word and if it conflicts with the pulpit of the church you are attending — deal with it. Confront the false teachings or leave the church and find another fellowship. If you listen to apostasy from the pulpit because the fellowship of others within that particular church is more important than God's Word — you are simply one of those folks that Jesus is referring to in Matthew 7:21-23.

Practice From The Heart

Jesus was very clear in his instructions: "If you want to enter into [eternal] life, keep the commandments." The rich young ruler says, "I have kept [these] from my youth." That means he is assured of eternal life! Notice that Jesus did not tell him that he must profess belief in the Son of God because he [Jesus] was the only way to receive eternal life. Why? Is it because Christ did not come for the righteous? Yes. He came for sinners.

Certainly, if this person kept God's commands, he was a righteous man in God's eyes. It is that simple and Jesus knew it. Try to understand this simple message from Jesus even if it goes against the grain of all your Christian programming. I know that you have been taught that no one can get into Heaven without Christ. This is a lie and part of the mythology. If you stick around long enough, I will guide you through those parts of God's Word that will make this fact clear to you. However, your understanding starts with these words of Jesus.

Note that Jesus also states in verse 17 that there is only ONE God that we serve. "No one is good but ONE, that is, God!"

This also may come as a shock. Yes, Jesus was the only human [in the flesh] begotten Son of God. Jesus stated clearly that the FATHER and he were one. I too will state this clearly for you. I too am one with the FATHER and Jesus. What we are talking about here is a spiritual oneness in which the FATHER's Spirit controls our life. Jesus never said that he was God, he only said he was here on God's (the FATHER's) business. That is, if you wanted to see the FATHER, all you had to do was look at his actions. The same can be said of any true believer that is led by God's Spirit. All real believers are going about the FATHER's business.

After he confirms he had kept God's commands since his youth, the rich young ruler asks the penetrating question: "What do I still lack?" What is it? It is the lack that everyone runs into when what you have in life is not enough to fill the emptiness that emanates from within your soul. As stated above, your money only gets you so far in terms of satisfying your soul. The bottle of booze or even drugs will only get you so far. No matter what you do or have in this earthly life, it will never be enough. There will always be a lack inside of your soul until you return to fellowship with the FATHER.

Practice From The Heart

___

Yes, God has put HIS laws in your mind and has written them on your heart. Fellowship with the FATHER is a matter of practice, practice, and practice. Specifically it is a matter of us getting back into the practice of fellowship with our heavenly FATHER. Jesus [and God's Holy Word] has made it very clear that you don't have to be perfect. But, you do have to try. You at least have to practice.

Jesus responds to the ruler's question with: "If you want to be perfect … do these things." The message is that nothing in your earthly habitat will make you perfect in God's eyes except selling it all off, giving it to the poor and following Jesus [God's direction]. It is a simple message. You should build up for yourself a treasure in Heaven. You should be friends with God and not of the earthly stuff. Yes, indeed you have to live here in the flesh. But, your heart and spirit can dwell with God in this earthly existence. That is the message from Jesus.

Jesus continues in verses 23-24 by pointing out how difficult it will be for a rich man to enter into Heaven. Remember that Jesus has already confirmed that this particular man will receive eternal life because he is keeping God's commandments. However, Jesus is now pointing out to his disciples the difficulties that a rich person will face. What Jesus is referring to here is that it is very difficult for rich people to give up their earthly possessions. That will become a major stumbling block for many. Why?

The danger in riches lies within the simple principle of control. With wealth you can easily have a feeling of controlling your own destiny. You hire things done for you and might even command an army of servants to do your bidding. With a focus on what you can do with your own resources, it is easy to lose sight of WHO allowed you to have those resources [wealth].

In 1993, I gave everything I own away. I gave up ownership in favor of stewardship. I no longer worry about money and assets. I let God worry about them for me. Whatever HE decides is fine with me. I can tell you that it was one of the best decisions I have ever made in my life. It helped move me from an earthly focus to a heavenly focus. While I still have huge goals in life, I am ever aware of this simple principle of control. God's Word says to lean not on your own understanding. That is what Jesus is talking about.

___

Copyright 2005 Edward G. Palmer, All Rights Reserved.

Book of Edward—Chapter 5

Practice From The Heart

___

Study God's Word and you will find that HE has loved murderers, adulterers and thieves. Name your sin here and you will find that God has loved all the sinners. Some of these people turned out to be great saints of the Bible. However, once they encountered God, they stopped the sinful behavior and entered into the practice of fellowshipping with the FATHER. You won't find God in fellowship with sin, wickedness, lawlessness and evil. Those Christians who think they can dwell in any of these areas are only deceiving themselves. They are certainly people Jesus is talking about in Matthew 7:21-23.

So we can observe throughout the Bible that our own perfection has never been a criterion of the FATHER. If it were, not a single soul would be saved. That leaves us only with the issue of practice. By now you might think I was way off base when I made the statement earlier that: "You reasoned correctly that God would not hold this particular lie against you."

I have used the illustration of lies for a couple of reasons. For one, lying comes quite easy to all of us. Often, our lying takes the form of not telling the whole truth of a matter. By withholding certain facts, we try to color the truth to get our own way. We rationalize that this is okay because official statistics tells us everyone lies an average of 25 times a day. Yes, I actually heard that bunk on a national network television show recently.

Let me ask you this question. Have you ever known someone who did not lie? If you are honest, you should have answered yes. If you couldn't answer yes, I suggest you find another church to attend and some new friends to associate with. Lying is not built within us as a default type of behavior; and, Apostle Paul is not an isolated case in history of someone who doesn't lie. It is not natural for anyone to lie his or her way through life. While it may come easy out of the mouth, lying takes a lot of effort to be clever enough to not get caught. Telling the truth is much easier and requires no memory bank or catalogue dedicated to deceit. People who practice lying have to work at it to be successful in this evil endeavor.

With God, a lie is a lie and there is no big or little lie. However, with God there are also those who "are lovers and practitioners of lies." These are clearly people who love to lie and think that they are very clever about it.

___

Copyright 2005 Edward G. Palmer, All Rights Reserved.

Practice From The Heart

The now infamous words of former president Clinton are illustrative of the principle God cites in Revelation 22:15. Who can ever forget: "It depends on what the word IS means. If this is the present tense of IS, then it means... if it is the past tense, it means." You get the picture. Then there is this statement before the entire nation: "I did not have sex with that woman." I want to be very clear about God's Word. These are statements from a "lover and practitioner of lies" and the Holy Spirit confirms this fact to me.

There are liars that God says are outside of the kingdom. They play around with the words in sentence structures to cloak or hide the truth. To get their own way. They know, like a lot of lawyers, the very same words of any given sentence can take on many different meanings by shifting the emphasis from one word in the sentence to another. Consider for the moment the following variations of Clinton's second statement. Read each sentence out loud and place an emphasis on the word in bold capital letters. See how the meaning of the sentence is changed by the word emphasized.

- I did not have sex with **THAT** woman.
- I did not have sex with that **WOMAN**.
- I did not have **SEX** with that woman.
- I did not **HAVE** sex with that woman.

It is a sad commentary today that our society now lends itself to the arrogance of such lies before a nation from a place of high honor. While people who lie can get away with deceiving other humans, God will know the truth of every situation. We cannot hide our lies from a heavenly FATHER who sees it all. I will leave it up to God to judge Mr. Clinton's repentant heart. Suffice to say that sincerity in this situation should not be an option.

The Nazi lie illustration is also similar to a biblical story. Let's now review the story of Rahab the harlot in Jericho. Rahab lied to the authorities to protect Jewish spies. What happened to her? What did God do to her? The story unfolds in the book of Joshua chapter 2. In my New King James Version, the story is titled: "The Faith of Rahab."

Practice From The Heart

The Faith Of Rahab

[1] "Now Joshua the son of Nun sent out two men from Acacia Grove to spy secretly, saying, 'Go, view the land, especially Jericho.' So they went, and came to the house of a harlot named Rahab, and lodged there."

[2] "And it was told the king of Jericho, saying, 'Behold, men have come here tonight from the children of Israel to search out the country.' [3] So the king of Jericho sent to Rahab, saying, 'Bring out the men who have come to you, who have entered your house, for they have come to search out all the country.' "

[4] "Then the woman took the two men and hid them.

[Rahab lies]

So she said, 'Yes, the men came to me, but I did not know where they were from. [5] And it happened as the gate was being shut, when it was dark that the men went out. Where the men went I do not know; pursue them quickly, for you may overtake them.' "

[6] "But she had brought them up to the roof and hidden them with the stalks of flax, which she had laid in order on the roof.

[7] Then the men pursued them by the road to the Jordan, to the fords. And as soon as those who pursued them had gone out, they shut the gate. [8] Now before they lay down, she came up to them on the roof, [9] and said to the men: 'I know that the LORD has given you the land, that the terror of you has fallen on us, and that all the inhabitants of the land are fainthearted because of you.' "

[10] "For we have heard how the LORD dried up the water of the Red Sea for you when you came out of Egypt, and what you did to the two kings of the Amorites who were on the other side of the Jordan, Sihon and Og, whom you utterly destroyed."

Copyright 2005 Edward G. Palmer, All Rights Reserved.

Book of Edward—Chapter 5

[11] "And as soon as we heard these things, our hearts melted; neither did there remain any more courage in anyone because of you, for the LORD your God, HE is God in Heaven above and on earth beneath."

[12] "Now therefore, I beg you, swear to me by the LORD, since I have shown you kindness, that you also will show kindness to my father's house, and give me a true token, and spare my father, my mother, my brothers, my sisters, and all that they have, and deliver our lives from death."

[14] "So the men answered her, 'Our lives for yours, if none of you tell this business of ours. And it shall be, when the LORD has given us the land, that we will deal kindly and truly with you.' "

[15] "Then she let them down by a rope through the window, for her house was on the city wall; she dwelt on the wall. [16] And she said to them, 'Get to the mountain, lest the pursuers meet you. Hide there three days, until the pursuers have returned. Afterward you may go your way.' "

[17] "So the men said to her: 'We will be blameless of this oath of yours which you have made us swear, unless, when we come into the land, you bind this line of scarlet cord in the window through which you let us down, and unless you bring your father, your mother, your brothers, and all your father's household to your own home.' "

[19] "So it shall be that whoever goes outside the doors of your house into the street, his blood shall be on his own head, and we will be guiltless. And whoever is with you in the house, his blood shall be on our head if a hand is laid on him."

[20] "And if you tell this business of ours, then we will be free from your oath which you made us swear."

Practice From The Heart

[21] "Then she said, 'According to your words, so be it.' And she sent them away, and they departed. And she bound the scarlet cord in the window. [22] They departed and went to the mountain, and stayed there three days until the pursuers returned. The pursuers sought them all along the way, but did not find them."

[23] "So the two men returned, descended from the mountain, and crossed over; and they came to Joshua the son of Nun, and told him all that had befallen them. [24] And they said to Joshua, 'Truly the LORD has delivered all the land into our hands, for indeed all the inhabitants of the country are fainthearted because of us.' " Joshua 2:1-24

> **"Now the city shall be doomed by the LORD to destruction, it and all who are in it. Only Rahab the harlot shall live, she and all who are with her in the house, because she hid the messengers that we sent." Joshua 6:17**

This is the very same kind of lie that was illustrated earlier in the Nazi example. God honored Rahab for protecting the Jews. Yes, God viewed Rahab's lie in a different light. It is a righteous thing to help God's people in their time of need and God will certainly reward those who do.

James reaffirms God's Word in James 2:25-26 stating: "Was not Rahab the harlot also justified by works when she received the messengers and sent them out another way? For as the body without the spirit is dead, so faith without works is dead also." Yes, this is another message that conflicts with modern day Christianity. Why?

Can we be perfect? The answer is clearly—No. But like Rahab, we can recognize God for who HE truly is. We can recognize HIS Holiness and righteousness. We can discern what really matters to HIM. We can give up and abandon our self-serving positions that rationalize our sinful life. We then enter into a relationship with HIM through fellowship. This, in turn, means that we keep HIS commandments and we practice certain things to demonstrate that we are part of the kingdom of God.

Practice From The Heart

What are these things we need to practice? What should we avoid practicing? The following list is not meant to be all-inclusive. Instead, it is a starting point. The kingdom of God is within you according to the words of Jesus. Make the most of it by now reviewing what you are practicing.

Practice & Do Not Practice Checklist!

- ✓ Practice the truth. 1 John 1:6
- ✓ Practice righteousness. 1 John 3:10
- ✓ Do not practice divination or soothsaying. Leviticus 19:26
- ✓ Do not practice wicked works. Psalm 141:4
- ✓ Do not practice ungodliness. Isaiah 32:6
- ✓ Do not practice divination. Ezekiel 13:23
- ✓ Do not practice lewdness. Ezekiel 23:48
- ✓ Do not practice iniquity or evil. Micah 2:1
- ✓ Do not practice lawlessness. Matthew 7:23
- ✓ Do not practice lesbianism. Romans 1:18-32
- ✓ Do not practice homosexuality. Romans 1:18-32
- ✓ Do not practice unrighteousness. Romans 1:18-32
- ✓ Do not practice lies. Romans 1:18-32; Revelation 22:15
- ✓ Do not practice envy. Galatians 5:21
- ✓ Do not practice drunkenness. Galatians 5:21
- ✓ Do not practice revelries. Galatians 5:21

Practice From The Heart

On two separate and distinct occasions this week, I was reminded of the story of Belshazzar in Daniel chapter 5. Perhaps, more than any other story in the Bible, this one illustrates why you need to pay attention to God. Why you need to practice truth and righteousness and why you need to avoid sin [as God has defined] in your life. Perfection? No. Practice? Yes!

The message came to me in such a way that I again simply "knew that God was speaking directly to me." He was speaking to me in a way that related to how I should end this chapter. The message started coming last Sunday evening as I pondered whether or not to go up town and see a late night movie. As I looked over the listing I debated which movie to see. My mind just needed a mental break and I have found that a good movie can be a great mental relaxation for me. I made some phone calls to find out what the movies were all about and after some consideration I decided to go see a movie entitled "A Knights Tale."

I enjoyed the movie and was struck by some unusual language during the course of the movie. The movie was about a peasant who wanted to be a Knight jousting with lances against other Knights. He got the opening and found himself competing against a very experienced "evil" Knight. During the first competition, the evil Knight won. The peasant said: "The next time … I will win." In response came the curious words: "I have measured and weighed you and found you wanting." The message was clear: "You don't stand a chance competing against me." The evil Knight repeated the same message to the peasant a couple of times. At the end of the movie, the evil Knight lost and the message was then repeated back to him. The whole dialogue was very interesting to me but I did not know why.

The next day [Monday], I was listening to a Bible teacher who was studying Daniel chapter 5 and the message came again to me from God through this teacher. It was God's response to Belshazzar. The essence of the message was: "You have been weighed on the scales and found wanting." [Daniel 5:27 NKJV] The Living Bible has a little more clarity.

> **"You have been weighed in God's balances and have failed the test!" Daniel 5:27 Living Bible**

Practice From The Heart

I spent some time studying it today and was astonished again by the message from God. Belshazzar was the son of Nebuchadnezzar and was now the ruling Babylonian king. He had a great feast in the company of a thousand. During the feast, he gave the command to fetch the gold and silver vessels, which his father had taken from God's temple in Jerusalem.

The king and his lords, his wives and his concubines drank wine from them and "praised the gods of gold and silver, bronze and iron, wood and stone." It literally incensed God who sent Belshazzar a direct message.

[5] "In the same hour the fingers of a man's hand appeared and wrote opposite the lampstand on the plaster of the wall of the king's palace; and the king saw the part of the hand that wrote."

[6] "Then the king's countenance changed, and his thoughts troubled him, so that the joints of his hips were loosened and his knees knocked against each other."

[7] "The king cried aloud to bring in the astrologers, the Chaldeans, and the soothsayers. The king spoke, saying to the wise men of Babylon, 'Whoever reads this writing, and tells me its interpretation, shall be clothed with purple and have a chain of gold around his neck; and he shall be the third ruler in the kingdom.'" Daniel 5:5-7

Imagine looking at the wall and seeing only the fingers of a hand, writing a message with no arm or body attached. This is what Belshazzar was witnessing. Verse 24 of Daniel 5 tells us that the fingers were sent from God. You might just feel a little sick yourself. I wrote earlier that God would take only so much from man. God has limits. This time, the king had crossed God's limit. How much mercy and grace will God display to you? I cannot say. I can only state that you had better get yourself straight with God and stay that way. That includes whether you claim to have Jesus or not. The principle is the same. God tolerates sin up to a certain point and then no more. Belshazzar had gone too far and God had responded with a message on the wall that none of his advisors could decipher. Now what?

Practice From The Heart

Turning to the New Century Version we see with clarity the message of God and its meaning. Daniel had to be called to decipher the meaning of the message for Belshazzar.

[25] "These are the words that were written on the wall: 'Mene, mene, tekel, and parsin.' "

[26] "This is what the words mean: Mene: God has counted the days until your kingdom will end."

[27] "Tekel: You have been weighed on the scales and found not good enough."

[28] "Parsin: Your kingdom is being divided and will be given to the Medes and Persians."

[30] "That very same night Belshazzar, king of the Babylonian people, was killed." Daniel 5:25-28, 30 NCV

Daniel 5 states that Belshazzar "was not sorry for what he had done" and that he had set himself "against the LORD of Heaven." Further that he "did not honor God, who has power over your life and everything you do."

I am wondering about you. Do you realize that we serve an awesome God that has expectations and limits despite any past programming? Do you realize that HE will stand by HIS Holy Word despite any Christian belief you have that might try to contradict it? In a "party" atmosphere or sheer moment in time, you may find that you also have crossed the line with God.

For Belshazzar this meant immediate death and an end to his earthly existence. He certainly wasn't Heaven bound either. This king set himself against the God of Heaven who has HIS own fixed values and definitions of what is right and what is wrong. What is good and what is evil? You might think that homosexuality or lesbianism is of God because it has a "love" component. However, you have simply perverted the ways of God by taking such a position. You have in fact crossed a line with God. Nothing in Jesus has changed the ways of God or the nature of the kingdom of God.

The lesson of Belshazzar should be heeded by all that call themselves a child of God [or Christian]. It is a lesson of obedience. It is a lesson of limits to God's grace. It is a lesson of an individual who felt they could do whatever they wanted to do despite what a holy God requires of us.

Today, in Christianity, many believe they can live exactly like king Belshazzar did. So, let the party begin? These Christians believe they can simply do their own thing without any fear of consequence from God. They have adopted a new more sin-friendly god who they call either the "god of forgiveness" or "the god of health/wealth" without realizing that the God of the Bible has not changed. Often they refer to one of these new gods as Jesus. In the process, the FATHER is insulted by a cheap grace that treats the blood of Jesus as a common thing. Has Jesus redefined God's nature? No.

Yes, our God has forgiveness. However, he expects fruit worthy of repentance. That fruit manifests itself in our behaviors and in our habits. What we do in life in terms of actions or lack of actions confirm to God exactly who we are. HE knows we can't be perfect, but fully expects that we can try. HE also fully expects that we practice doing good and not evil.

Getting back into fellowship with the FATHER means practice from our heart in a way that conforms us to God's Holy Word and HIS idea of right and wrong, not the other way around. It means that we have reached a point in humility where we understand that it is God who really controls our life. You know that there is more to life than what your senses and intellect can discern. Just look at the wonder of God on this earth wherever you turn. No matter what you acquire on this earth and the resources you have, you will ultimately reach the point that the rich ruler reached and ask yourself, "What do I lack?" That is when you will know it is time for some practice from the heart, because that results in true fellowship with God Almighty!

Fellowship With The FATHER, Means That You ...
Practice From The Heart

Chapter Six
The Heart of an Apostle

"A servant of Jesus Christ, called to be an apostle, separated unto the gospel of God." Romans 1:1 KJV

"Called to be an apostle of Jesus Christ through the will of God." 1 Cor. 1:1 KJV

"An apostle, not of men, neither by man, but by Jesus Christ, and God the FATHER, who raised him from the dead."
Gal 1:1 KJV

"An apostle of Jesus Christ by the will of God, to the saints which are at Ephesus, and to the faithful in Christ."
Eph. 1:1 KJV

"An apostle of Jesus Christ by the commandment of God our Saviour, and Lord Jesus Christ, which is our hope."
1 Tim. 1:1 KJV

"Whereunto I am ordained a preacher, and an apostle … a teacher of …" 1 Tim. 2:7 KJV

"Wherefore, holy brethren, partakers of the heavenly calling, consider the *apostle* and High Priest of our profession, Christ Jesus." Hebrews 3:1 KJV

"A servant and an apostle … to them that have obtained like precious faith with us through the righteousness of God and our Saviour Jesus Christ." 2 Peter 1:1 KJV

The Heart of an Apostle

Many months have passed since I wrote Chapter 5. For many including me, life has been very difficult following the attacks of 9/11. However, this last Tuesday, God helped me to resume the writing of this book. God willing, it will be finished this year in a timely manner.

It doesn't surprise me that God also arranged the events of this week. And, of course, like the preceding five chapters, God is in the process of altering and reorganizing the contents of this chapter far from what I had originally thought. I have learned to go with the flow of God's Spirit and yield to God's "inspiration!" That is, in part, what it means to have the heart of an apostle. Yielding to God means HIS thoughts are more important than yours. It also means that HIS words are more important than yours.

This last week, God focused my attention on the word "repent", the King James Bible (KJV) and the issue of infallibility. Just three nights ago on Wednesday, we studied the issue of "infallibility" at length. It wasn't the first time. Do you believe that the Bible is infallible? That it contains no errors? That is, it is an inerrant guide from God? Note: The majority of the verses cited in this chapter are from the King James Bible in accordance with instructions I have received from God for this subject.

On Thursday night [two nights ago], God also provided the final points of discussion for this chapter at a contentious public Bible study I chose to attend. It was hosted by another small group of God's truth seekers. They are like the people who study and worship with me. They are called to set aside prior doctrinal teachings of the Christian Church and to ferret out the truth from God's Holy Word based only upon Scripture. Like the Bereans did with the teachings of Apostle Paul, we search the Scriptures and test all teachings against the written word of God.

> **"These [from Berea] were more noble than those in Thessalonica, in that they [actually] received the word with all readiness of mind, and searched the Scriptures daily, [testing] whether those things [taught] were so [true]."**
> **Acts 17:11 KJV**

The Heart of an Apostle

Why would you want to search the Scriptures yourself? You too need to test the teachings of your church, just like the Bereans tested Paul's teachings. Becoming knowledgeable in the Scriptures means that you will not be led astray by the errant doctrines of mankind. Many congregations are manipulated by the false teachings from the pulpit. However, your church will not be judged as a unit before God. Instead, each individual in the church including you are responsible for his or her own sin. How do you know what is acceptable and unacceptable to God? How do you know what is sin [the activities you want to stop]? It comes from reading God's Word.

"All Scripture is given by inspiration of God, and is profitable for doctrine, for reproof, for correction, for instruction in righteousness." 2 Tim. 3:16 KJV

"Study to shew thyself approved unto God, a workman that needeth not to be ashamed, rightly dividing the word of truth." 2 Tim. 2:15 KJV

While the King James Bible is widely used, the language is very stilted and we no longer speak the King's English. Modern translations can present God's Word in a more easy to understand fashion. For example, the New King James Bible presents 2 Timothy 2:15 as follows:

"Be diligent to present yourself approved to God, a worker who does not need to be ashamed, rightly dividing the word of truth." 2 Tim. 2:15 NKJV

Depending upon your loyalty to the King James Bible, you may or may not agree that the NKJV better presents the above verse. In any case, God's Word is clear that you need to study it. Today, it is estimated that only 15% of those who claim to be Christians are actually students of the Bible. If you are not one of the 15%, then I must warn you that you cannot appreciate the grave danger you and your family may be involved in when it comes to Christian mythology. Without a working understanding of the Bible, you are ignorant. Ignorance can be "bliss" on the earth, but you will have no excuses for your sin before God at the time of your judgment.

The Heart of an Apostle

Four contentious young men who claimed to be filled with the Holy Spirit also attended Thursday night's public Bible study. Their insulting behavior and divisiveness illustrated the words of Jesus when he said: "You will know them by their fruits." What are the fruits of the Spirit?

"But the fruit of the Spirit is love, joy, peace, longsuffering, gentleness, goodness, faith." Galatians 5:22 KJV

"For the fruit of the Spirit is in all goodness and righteousness and truth." Ephesians. 5:9 KJV

The Bible also contrasts the fruits of the flesh. Consider the following Bible verses:

"Now the works of the flesh are manifest, which are these; Adultery, fornication, uncleanness, lasciviousness, idolatry, witchcraft, hatred, variance, emulations, wrath, strife, seditions, heresies, envyings, murders, drunkenness, revellings, and such like: of the which I tell you before, as I have also told you in time past, that they which do such things shall not inherit the kingdom of God."
                                             Galatians 5:19-21 KJV

Among the fruits of the flesh exhibited by the truth squad on Thursday night were idolatry, wrath, strife and heresies. There was also a lack of peace and goodness. Gentleness was not in their arsenal as they insisted repeatedly it was their right to "contend for their faith." Not in a new group of people without taking the time to know them and what they stand for! To this apostle, it was witnessing sheer arrogance and ungodly behavior.

I am mindful of the gentleness of Jesus when he dealt with sinners. Jesus never beat people into submission from Scripture with strong rhetoric. That is something to think about. Why didn't he? It is all about free will. In direct contrast to those modern day teachings about beating people into salvation, God is the ONE who calls us unto HIM.

The Heart of an Apostle

If God calls us, you can surmise that HE doesn't call everyone. No matter what you believe, some people are predestined for evil just like Judas Iscariot. If God wants everyone saved, why wasn't Judas Iscariot saved? After all, he was in close and direct fellowship with Jesus Christ. The answer is now overlooked by many of the aggressive elements within Christianity and it is very simple. God respects every person's free will. We are told to preach the Word. However, we are not told to beat sinners into salvation with our rhetoric.

God Respects Your Free Will!

> **"He that is unjust, let him be unjust still: and he which is filthy, let him be filthy still: and he that is righteous, let him be righteous still: and he that is holy, let him be holy still."**
> **Rev. 22:11 KJV**

If those who claim to be of God and "filled with HIS Spirit" fully understood this, there would be no rhetorical attempts to coerce sinners into salvation. The old adage is still true: "A man convinced against his will is of the same opinion still." Aggressive salvation workers need to remember <u>first</u> the gentleness of Christ; <u>second</u>, that God has not called everyone to salvation either with Christ or without Christ; and <u>third</u>, that God respects man's [or woman's] free will to choose. Even to choose eternal damnation over eternal life. Many, so-called Christians, have never made a free will choice from their heart for God. Have you? If not, isn't it time—right now?

When you have the heart of an apostle, you understand the above three factors. You understand that God wants to get HIS word out so a free will choice can "be better understood." However, HE does not want you to go armed with a "truth squad" and rifles. Not Christians, Jews or Muslims!

> **"Nevertheless the foundation of God standeth sure, having this seal, the LORD knoweth them that are HIS. And, let every one that nameth the name of Christ depart from iniquity [stop practicing lawlessness]." 2 Tim. 2:19 KJV**

The Heart of an Apostle

An armed "truth squad" dedicated to their King James Bible describes the aggressive four men at Thursday night's Bible study. They were intent on saving everyone. They presumed, like a lot of Christian warriors, that everyone must need to be saved because they did not believe what they believed. They may also believe that anyone who uses an English Bible other than the King James Bible is in total error.

There is a movement in society today that takes such a stance. They even infer that anyone who uses the New King James Bible is of the devil. They believe this because of the ancient trinity symbol used on the NKJV. To them, the ancient trinity symbol represents a graphic of the number 666. The ultimate apostasy is to try and improve the King James Bible. I can tell you that this confusion, itself, is evidence of the work of the Antichrist. Those who attempt to shut down an honest debate over Scripture and its various translations are NOT OF GOD. They are, of the Antichrist. Remember Isaiah 1:18 where God says: "Come and let us reason together?" Those who walk with God are gentle people who can be reasoned with.

I have studied the New King James Bible for over 20 years. But, I have not studied it alone. I use over 19 different Bibles. A full 12 or more of them are on computer software where the Bible text is easily searched for truth. At all of our Bible studies, we have at least one or more King James Bible open. We also have one or two parallel Bibles open. Each of these has four translations side by side. At a minimum then, our studies have six (6) different Bible translations open for constant comparison.

When I asked the young men some questions, there were some curious issues exposed. One issue was that of the word "iniquity." They did not understand that it also translates as lawlessness. Compare the KJV and NKJV of Matthew 7:23.

> **"And then will I profess unto them, I never knew you: depart from me, ye that work iniquity." Matthew 7:23 KJV**

> **"And then I will declare to them, I never knew you: depart from me, you who practice lawlessness."**
> **Matthew 7:23 NKJV**

Copyright 2005 Edward G. Palmer, All Rights Reserved.

The Heart of an Apostle

In the above verses, you can see that the KJV renders the words "ye that work iniquity" and that the NKJV translates this as "you who practice lawlessness."

From Strong'S® Concordance, we see that the word "iniquity" in the above KJV verse is derived from the Greek word ***anomia***, which is pronounced an-om-ee'-ah. It means illegality, i.e. violation of law or (gen) wickedness: - iniquity, X transgress (-ion of) the law, unrighteousness.

Therefore, both translations render the Greek word appropriately. Yet, isn't the NKJV easier to understand? On Thursday night, the four salvation warriors did not understand the NJKV translation nor did they understand the meaning of lawlessness. It was simply not in their vernacular. To put it bluntly, they were entrenched within the language of the KJV and within the doctrine of the assembly they came from. They were also not equipped to rightly divide the word of God as all are charged to do. They were, instead, equipped with rhetorical machinations designed to beat sinners into salvation. They were also steeped in a very interesting doctrine on *"perfection"* that got my attention.

They believed it is impossible for real believers to sin in any form after receiving salvation through Christ. They believed you are then perfect just like Christ. It was interesting for me as I was preparing to write this chapter. Little did I know that God would provide more input to me as he rearranged my life this last week. This perfection doctrine dovetails quite nicely with Chapter 5 and it needs to be discussed at this time.

You recall that I ended Chapter 5 with the admonishment that God expects us to live a sin free life. Inasmuch as is humanly possible having His Spirit inside of us. You also recall the prior discussions on Hebrews 10:26. The King James Bible renders the translation of this verse as follows:

"For if we sin wilfully after that we have received the knowledge of the truth, there remaineth no more sacrifice for sins." Hebrews 10:26 KJV

The Heart of an Apostle

Therefore, even the King James Bible acknowledges and distinguishes that there exists a condition called "willful sin." Intellectually, it doesn't take much to surmise that there then must also be a condition called unwillful sin. What could that be? It could be sin that you are not even aware of or even simply unintended sin. These two types of sin were cited earlier in the chapter on repentance [page 44]. God's Word makes it clear to us that even if we are unaware of our sins, HE will still hold us accountable for them. However, Christ is our propitiation for those types of sin for God.

Christ is not a blanket that covers a life of wickedness. However, his blood does cover "unknown and unintentional" types of sin for us. Yes, it means that we are not 100% perfect on our own as the Thursday night truth squad tried to assert. The moderator shouted back: "That's blasphemy!" Few things are tantamount to this. However, the idea that we become 100% *"perfect"* [instantly] in the sense these men postulated is indeed blasphemy.

> **"Be ye therefore perfect, even as your FATHER which is in Heaven is perfect." Matthew 5:48 KJV**
>
> **"The disciple is not above his master: but every one that is perfect shall be as his master." Luke 6:40 KJV**
>
> **"I in them, and THOU in me, that they may be made perfect in ONE; and that the world may know that THOU hast sent me, and hast loved them, as THOU hast loved me."**
> **John 17:23 KJV**
>
> **"Whom we preach, warning every man, and teaching every man in all wisdom; that we may present every man perfect [to God] in Christ Jesus." Col. 1:28 KJV**
>
> **"So everywhere we go we talk about Christ to all who will listen, warning them and teaching them as well as we know how. We want to be able to present each one to God, perfect because of what Christ has done for each of them."**
> **Col. 1:28 Living**

Copyright 2005 Edward G. Palmer, All Rights Reserved.

Book of Edward—Chapter 6

The Heart of an Apostle

If your doctrine says that we can be perfect through Christ Jesus in the eyes of God, then I fully agree. If, instead, the doctrine says we are perfect per se' [in and of ourselves after accepting Christ], then the doctrine is false and fails to understand how the grace of God actually works within our newborn souls. Such a doctrine acknowledges John's words in 1 John 3:9-10 but fails to understand the ramifications of Paul's words in Romans 7:19.

When I pointed out "unknown and unintentional" sin to the truth squad, they dismissed the Old Testament as being irrelevant. However, if you have the heart of an apostle, you understand that the Old Testament remains true today and that God has not changed. You also understand from your heart that the New Testament cannot be fully understood without first understanding the Old Testament. Was God Almighty changed when Jesus Christ arrived? When Christ was crucified? Not according to Malachi 3:6.

Another problem posed for the truth squad on Thursday was that the very idea of "lawlessness" implies you have to obey God's laws. Their doctrine seemed to dismiss God's laws. The word "practice" also does not show up in the vernacular of the King James Bible and, of course, it does run counter to their doctrine and idea of "instantly becoming 100% perfect."

We can look at Moses who walked with God daily and marched the Israelites out of Egypt. Since Moses was in direct contact with God and walked with HIM, can we surmise that perfection was in Moses? No, and Moses is a prime example of what our lives will be like walking with God. Moses struck a rock prematurely for water and it angered God. He made an error in judgment. Such error prone behavior is the nature of our human existence, even when we walk very closely with our God.

We are not 100% perfect on our own accord. Yet, we can choose to make righteous choices to honor God each and every day of our lives. We understand what "Thou shalt not" means. And, we don't. God's laws are obvious and meaningful to us and we don't think twice about obeying them. Indeed, God's law is written on our hearts and placed in our minds. Having accepted God and his Son Jesus, we carry "HIS brand." We belong to God.

The Heart of an Apostle

However, like Moses, human errors in judgment and even getting confronted with potential sin happen all the time, every day. Our job is to pick up the cross daily and to choose each day to be all that we can be for God. The heart of an apostle strives to make righteous choices because he or she understands they have to or otherwise they do not belong to God. The heart of an apostle will not willfully sin. The heart of the apostle will trust in God to guide him or her through life's minefield. And, should they find themselves unwittingly involved in some kind of sin, they will confront that sin as soon as it is humanly recognized. The heart of an apostle knows he or she can become 99% perfect. Practice to 99%—yes; Perfect to 100% —no!

As we walk with God daily and as our knowledge of God's Word gains depth, our spiritual discernment increases. As our spiritual knowledge and discernment increase, we will become more perfect in God's eyes by the day and by the minute. As you make more and more right choices based upon God's Word, your spiritual strength will become strong. The stronger you get, the closer to God you get. The closer to God you get and the more active you demonstrate your faith, the more of a target you will make yourself to the enemies of God. Hence, the more of Christ's strength you will need in your life. Satan doesn't care about "so-called Christians" who don't stand up for righteousness. Why is that? They're into myths not God.

> **"And he said unto me, MY grace is sufficient for thee: for MY strength is made perfect in weakness." 2 Cor. 12:9 KJV**

> **"For though I would desire to glory, I shall not be a fool; for I will say the truth: but now I forbear, lest any man should think of me above that which he seeth me to be, or that he heareth of me." 2 Cor. 12:6 KJV**

With the assurance of salvation in your life, you need to adopt the heart of an apostle. A heart like Paul who writes: "Lest any man think of me above that which he seeth me to be, or that he heareth of me." Paul understood his job was to glorify God, not himself. Yet, in these last days, men are boasters of themselves. Indeed, they see themselves 100% perfect in every way. Even on the same level with God as Satan saw himself.

The Heart of an Apostle

In Christ, We Are Perfect In God's Eyes!

The truth squad at Thursday's meeting started to badger the moderator. One would ask a question. But, before it could be answered, another would chime in with the next question. The dialogue became interesting to me when one young man asked the moderator: "Are you a sinner?" The moderator responded, as I would have at the time, with YES. Of course, the response was just what the rhetorical questioner wanted. The truth squad expounded on 1 John 3:9-10 and without giving the moderator any chance to respond, they assumed he and everyone else were unsaved.

I sensed what was going on from this team and I asked the moderator: "Are you a willful sinner?" He responded NO. Just like I would have. The next hour was quite contentious as the team of four young men took on the attitude that "Praise Jesus, we have located a den of seven sinners." That was the rest of us who actually came to study the Bible. However, if these young men had learned some manners with their rhetorical skills, they would have found out otherwise. The moderator finally asked: "Why are you here?" The answer was: "We are here to save [your] souls."

Later I realized how clever these young men were with their tactics. If someone admits to being a sinner, they must be unsaved. That was the logic of their perfection doctrine. The answer from the moderator was never allowed to be clarified and his and the perspective of everyone else was:

"If we say that we have not sinned, we make him a liar, and his word is not in us." 1 John 1:10 KJV

Their "perfect" theology rhetorically split hairs. John writes if anyone says he has not sinned, he is a liar. Their point from 1 John 3:9-10 was that now, after Christ, you should be spiritually and humanly 100% sin free. Now let's go back to John in 1 John 3:9-10 and Paul in Romans 7:19 and carefully examine whether the Bible supports this 100% perfection doctrine.

Apostles John & Paul Clarify Sin!

"Whosoever is born of God doth not commit sin; for His seed remaineth in him: and he cannot sin, because he is born of God. In this the children of God are manifest, and the children of the devil: whosoever doeth not righteousness is not of God, neither he that loveth not his brother."
1 John 3:9-10 KJV

"Whoever has been born of God does not sin, for His seed remains in him; and he cannot sin, because he has been born of God. In this the children of God and the children of the devil are manifest: Whoever does not practice righteousness is not of God, nor is he who does not love his brother." 1 John 3:9-10 NKJV

Apostle John was trying to get the point across for God that you simply cannot go around in life willfully sinning if you claim Christ as your savior. Real believers have a duty to God to walk a straight and narrow path with God. Indeed, real [sincere] believers have no problem with this since the Spirit of God flows inside of them. John continues his dialogue with the idea of doing righteousness as a sign of the believer not sinning. The NKJV translates "doeth not righteousness" into "does not practice righteousness," which is well supported by the Greek word *poieo*, pronounced poy-eh'-o as shown in Strong'S® Concordance.

Therefore, if you have a proper understanding of Apostle John, you would demonstrate your sinless [almost perfect] life to God by [practicing] righteousness. Our acts of righteousness are defined by doing what is right in the eyes of God, not in the eyes of man. You also cannot understand Apostle John if you don't understand Apostle Paul. Likewise, you cannot understand any apostle unless you first understand the Apostle Jesus Christ.

The Heart of an Apostle

Those with the heart of an apostle respect the words of Christ and "take them to heart." The heart of an apostle understands that Jesus Christ spoke directly for God and said only what God told him to say. Further, they understand that Christ only did what God told him to do. To deny the words and deeds of Jesus Christ is to deny God Almighty HIMSELF. It is the work of the Antichrist that alters the plain words of Christ in Christianity.

Apostles don't try to explain away Christ's words and in the process make Christ a liar. Either what the Apostle Jesus Christ told us is truth or it isn't. The words of Jesus cannot simply be dismissed because they run counter to any man made Christian doctrine or theology. Any doctrine or theology that has the effect of negating the words of Jesus Christ is NOT FROM GOD. It is that simple. Further, any fellowship of so-called Christians that do not obey Christ and accept his words at face value do not belong to Jesus Christ. They will be part of those whom Christ informs at the time of judgment: "I never knew you." When asked to accept the words of Jesus, the truth squad denied Christ. In the process of refusing to accept what Christ said, they made Christ out to be a liar. More in a moment, but for now, let's get back to Apostle Paul in Romans. Paul writes:

> **"For the good that I would I do not: but the evil which I would not, that I do. Now if I do that I would not, it is no more I that do it, but sin that dwelleth in me. I find then a law, that, when I would do good, evil is present with me. For I delight in the law of God after the inward man: But I see another law in my members, warring against the law of my mind, and bringing me into captivity to the law of sin which is in my members. O wretched man that I am! Who shall deliver me from the body of this death? I thank God through Jesus Christ our Lord. So then with the mind I myself serve the law of God; but with the flesh the law of sin." Romans 7:19-25 KJV**

Paul laments that a war wages within him between the flesh and the spirit. The more you exercise your spiritual muscles, the more your flesh will become subjected to the will of your spirit.

The Heart of an Apostle

I have walked with God now for over 25 years. I walked with HIM for 20 years before I received HIS call of apostleship. I also ignored the call for at least 2 years. I am sure that I was not saved during the first 32 years of my life. God was all head knowledge to me. The matters of the heart that I now speak to you about did not exist for me in the first 32 years of my life.

Most of us know someone whom the following statement applies: "He [or she] doesn't seem to have a heart for his [or her] job." When someone doesn't have a heart for their job, they don't seem to do it very well. They are disheartened. When I talk of having a heart for God, the opposite is true. You are excited to learn more about God. You study HIS Holy Bible. You get excited about fellowshipping with other believers. And, like Jesus proclaimed, you worship only God "In Spirit and truth." The issue of our sin can be further clarified with this graphic.

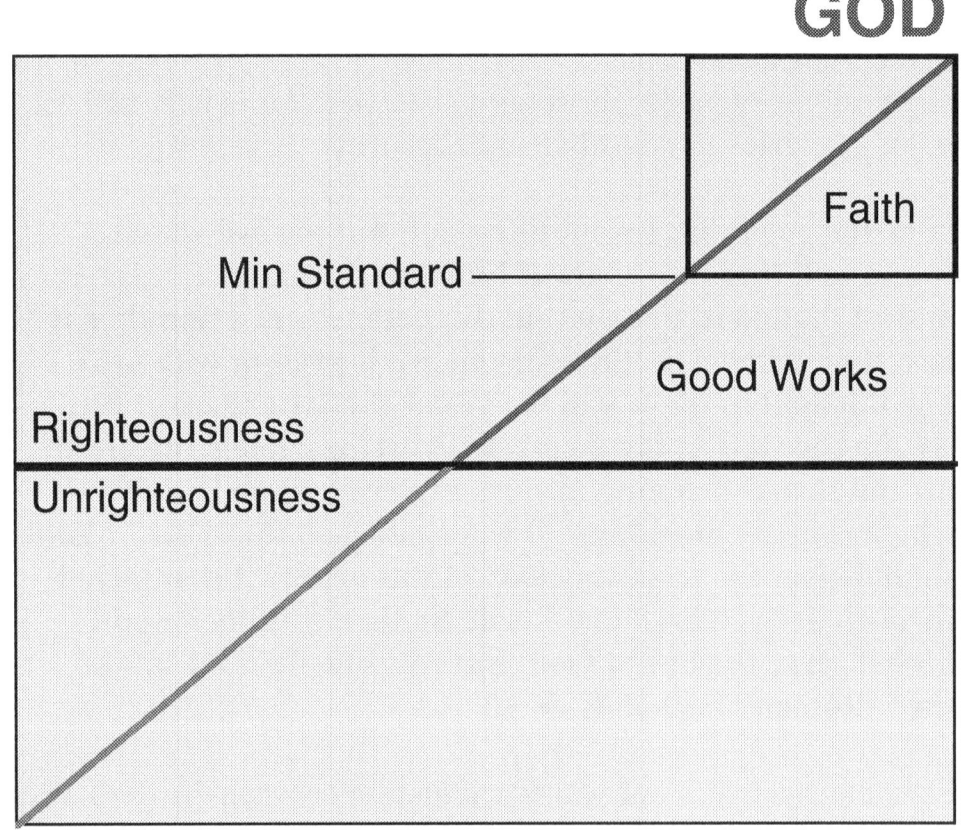

The Heart of an Apostle

Good works alone doesn't get people into Heaven. When Jesus proclaimed: "I never knew you," it wasn't because those Christians hadn't done something good. Listen to their response.

> **"Many will say to me in that day, Lord, Lord, have we not prophesied in thy name? And in thy name have cast out devils? And in thy name done many wonderful works?"**
> **Matthew 7:22 KJV**

It takes a bold person to prophesy in the name of Christ. It takes a bold person to cast out devils in the name of Christ. It takes a bold person to do many wonderful works in the name of Christ. Yet, all of this can get you nothing. Why? Jesus tells us why with: "Get away from me you who work iniquity; you who practice lawlessness."

The graphic on page 106 is an image God gave me this morning as I awoke. If you want to understand the nuances between good works and faith, it is a good starting point. It is not meant to be all-inclusive and it shouldn't be taken as such. However, consider that Christ has informed us that there exists a minimum righteousness standard. He also indicated that the scribes and Pharisees didn't make the cut. Listen to the words of Christ.

> **"For I say unto you, that except your righteousness shall exceed the righteousness of the scribes and Pharisees, ye shall in no case enter into the kingdom of Heaven."**
> **Matthew 5:20 KJV**

Hear the plain word from Christ that informs you that your own righteousness will play a factor in your salvation. Then, recognize that Christ's words are opposite to a lot of Christian doctrine today. The graph above is separated into two halves. Above the centerline is righteousness and below the line is unrighteousness. A diagonal line represents the continuum between Satan at the bottom and God at the top. The deeper your unrighteousness is, the closer you are to Satan. Likewise, the stronger your righteousness is, the closer you are to God.

Copyright 2005 Edward G. Palmer, All Rights Reserved.

The Heart of an Apostle

When Jesus told us why those Christians didn't make it in Matthew 7:22, he said they were practicing lawlessness. Those people cast out by Christ were working both sides of the fence. In other words, while it is true they did good things, they also demonstrated no respect for God because they also operated on the unrighteous turf of Satan. Fellowshipping with Satan in the works of unrighteousness means that they never really received God's call. There is no fence with God. Once saved, we cannot go back to the world of willful sin. We have to make the conscious choice daily to walk with God sin free [99%]. When we do error, our sin is miniscule compared to what it would be without Christ. If I were to overlay the sin graphic from page 43 onto this second sin graphic, it would look like this.

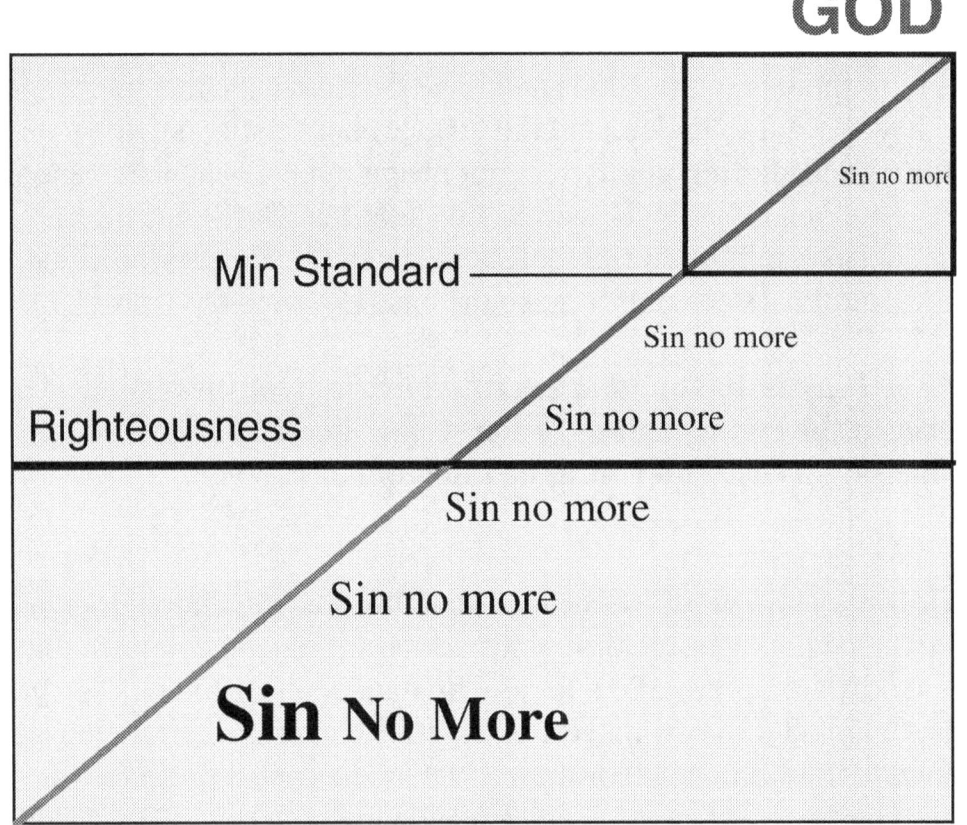

The Heart of an Apostle

Walking with God means you quickly jump up into the square in the upper right. That is where you operate in your new life of righteousness. It is far away from the world of sin. It is the realm of faith. Faith is exercised by unyielding will power dedicated to truth and righteousness. You understand fully that you CANNOT BE PERFECT 100% on your own. You understand that you need both God the FATHER's Spirit and the spirit of Christ within you just to live up to the expectations that God has for you. You no longer lean on your own understanding because you now know that God's ways are higher than man's way. Without HIS Spirit and the spirit of Christ inside of you, you realize that you would meet with failure. That is because you have developed the heart of an apostle; a heart that loves God and understands it is HE <u>and</u> Christ within us that help us to be obedient.

After you gave your heart to God, you either instantaneously or within a short time literally dumped all the sinful behavior that falls below the line of righteousness. You realize that you need to practice righteousness all the time. When the unrighteous behavior of colleagues, family and friends surface, you have no problem letting them know why you choose not to participate. Your life becomes a living testament for God and Christ. Because you know that God has a minimum righteousness standard, you quickly dump the rest of your routine sinful behavior including the bad habits you've acquired from the world and you operate in the area of *Faith*.

Your Heart Speaks Loudly To God!

When it comes to sin, your heart will matter more to God than any perceived notion that you failed to be 100% perfect and 100% sin free. When Peter denied Jesus three times to the authorities, did he sin? Yes, to me, that was sin. That is the level of sin that comes from the understanding of the heart of an apostle. Yet, Peter did not deny his God. The Almighty God and HIS only begotten Son that I know will use your weakness to demonstrate their strength. Their compassion on us mere humans will cover our shortcomings. All this occurs for the person who will walk a life of faith with God.

The Heart of an Apostle

The badgering at Thursday's Bible study bordered on intimidation when the truth squad launched the next serious question. "Who appointed you a teacher? Which apostle appointed you? You know that the Bible makes it clear that only an apostle can appoint a teacher?" The emphasis of these four young men could not have been clearer. They specifically challenged the moderator's credentials and his right to lead a Bible study. Who exactly are you to open your Bible and guide others in a study? That was the unmistakable attitude and it disturbed everyone.

Did apostles only appoint teachers? Exactly what was their Bible reference? Since they never offered any proof Scriptures for this doctrine, I will never know their exact reasoning. However, I know their claims are not in Scripture because the word of God states clearly:

"And God hath set some in the church, first apostles, secondarily prophets, thirdly teachers, after that miracles, then gifts of healings, helps, governments, diversities of tongues." 1 Cor. 12:28 KJV

Want to know who commissioned the moderator to lead that Bible study on Thursday night? It was God Almighty. Want to know who commissioned me to become an apostle? It was God Almighty. There are no Scriptures in the King James Bible that state apostles appoint teachers. One can only conclude that theirs was a man made doctrine. It has no basis in God's Word. How exactly does God set these people in the church? God sets them inside the church by the call on their hearts. In other words, God speaks to their hearts in a way that they get the message, even if they get the message reluctantly at first. So, do they all voluntarily jump into the shoes of any of these offices just because God calls? I doubt it. Like the Prophet Jonah and the Apostle Paul, God made it plain to them through various means that this is what HE wanted them to do.

God Almighty said: "I have an offer you can't refuse." Does it sound familiar?

The Heart of an Apostle

Whether it is reluctant or voluntarily, it is God Almighty that sorts out the qualifications of the individual for each office. HE knows what you are capable of even if you don't realize it. Moses is the classic example of the person who initially said: "Not me, I think you need someone else. Why, I can't even speak straight." You know the rest of the story.

God Calls The Apostles, Prophets And Teachers!

The arrogance of the truth squad on Thursday seemed to be also attached to their King James Bible. I can say that because they seemed totally ignorant of the translated language in other versions.

Is the King James English translation the "inerrant" word of God? The "infallible" word of God, which is another way of saying that it, has no errors within it? Considerable debate is taking place on this various issue. However, supporting such a doctrine must come from uninformed people. Well, at least from people who do not have the KJV text on their computer for fast and easy searching of truth? It would certainly have to come from those who do not have parallel translations along with a Hebrew and Greek dictionary.

What we know about the King James Bible is that it was at least the 15th translation of the Bible that occurred. There were many Bibles before it, including English translations, and many after it. Some of those that support the exclusive use of the King James Bible hold to the belief that it is not only inspired, it is also inerrant. Critics of the King James Bible would point out that earlier versions of many manuscripts were found later. Convention holds that those earlier translations would be more accurate since less time had passed from the original writings. They would also point out that the language of the King James Bible is out of date and no longer easily understood by English speaking people.

I have seen verses in the King James Bible that speak so wonderfully to a particular subject. Then, there are those you would need to study very carefully and ponder a long time simply because the language is so stilted.

The Heart of an Apostle

The New King James Bible seeks to retain the eloquence of the original King James Bible translation. However, it also seeks to clear up the language issues and translation errors found from the newly available earlier manuscripts of Scripture. Since I am exposed to both constantly, I can attest to the validity of the New King James Bible. It is easy to read and it has an accurate translation of the original biblical text. The doctrinal statement at the back of this book has been closely examined using the King James Bible (KJV), the New King James Bible (NKJV) and the New International Bible (NIV). I can tell you that all three versions support the doctrines described. Therefore, if you are partial to a certain translation and think you can summarily ignore all others, don't think for a moment it will matter with God. HE will still hold you accountable for searching out HIS truth.

It was last week when God had me search the word "repent" in the various translations. It is, for those supporters of an inerrant King James Bible, a very serious consequence. I suspect God showed me it so that the point can be made that all translations should be used to ferret out HIS truth. I would add the caveat that some newer translations should be held suspect in the sense of gender neutralization and other questionable practices. With modern computer technology, publishers can alter the text and mislead people quite easily.

Look for the activist homosexual and lesbian crowd to come up with their own Bible. They seriously need one that supports their sexual deviancy because they won't get that kind of support from God's Holy Word. Look for feminists to do so likewise. They could use one to support their cause of co-equalness with man in all respects. They too won't get such support from God's Holy Word because God has distinct callings on men and women, callings that compliment one another for HIS glory. Gender neutralization can only lead to further translation errors. Suffice to say, we have many excellent translations today and they all speak the same language. I would be wary of any new English translation with a specific goal in mind other than the exact translation of original biblical manuscripts.

Exactly how many English translations do we need?

The Heart of an Apostle

So, what about the infallibility issue of the King James Bible? The quick and easy answer is that it contains some errors. Having said that, most likely all other translations contain some errors. If you were looking for perfection, you missed the dialogue I offered on 99%. My guess is that all translations are at that 99% level. Many modern translations offer an excellent comparison against the King James Scripture. You most certainly need at least three translations if you are a serious student of the Bible.

Has God any reason to repent? Does God wreak evil upon people? Or, is His holy wrath justified by a need for justice? The answers seem very clear from the Bible.

> **"Every good gift and every perfect gift is from above, and cometh down from the FATHER of lights, with whom is no variableness, neither shadow of turning." James 1:17 KJV**

> **"God is not a man, that HE should lie; neither the son of man, that HE should repent: hath HE said, and shall HE not do it? Or hath HE spoken, and shall HE not make it good?"**
> **Numbers 23:19 KJV**

The KJV Bible is clear in James that all good things come from God. Then, in Numbers, the KJV Bible is also clear that God does not repent. Please note also that James asserts that there is "no variableness" with God meaning God does not change. Note also that Numbers states clearly that God will do exactly what HE says HE will do.

Conflict arises in the King James Bible when you examine the word repent. Not only does the King James Bible state accurately that God does not have anything to repent of, it later states that God DOES repent. What does God *repent* of? EVIL! Consider the following King James verses:

> **"For the LORD shall judge HIS people, and repent HIMSELF for HIS servants, when HE seeth that their power is gone, and there is none shut up, or left." Deut. 32:36 KJV**

The Heart of an Apostle

In the above verse, the King James Bible has God *repenting* for HIS servants. Contrast the New King James, which says: "God will have compassion on HIS servants." A Bible that states OPPOSITE conditions is not inerrant. You cannot on one hand state that God does not repent and then a few pages later start providing a list of how God does repent.

The King James Bible Has Errors!

"And also the STRENGTH of Israel will not lie nor repent: for HE is not a man, that HE should repent."
1 Samuel 15:29 KJV

In the above verse, we see once again that the King James Bible clearly states that: "God [Strength of Israel] does not repent."

"For the LORD will judge HIS people, and HE will repent HIMSELF concerning HIS servants." Psalm 135:14 KJV

In the above verse, we see once again that the King James Bible has God *repenting* for HIS servants. Contrast the New King James, which again says HE will have compassion on HIS servants. This isn't too complicated here. Do you think that God will repent for HIS servants or have compassion on them?

"If that nation, against whom I have pronounced, turn from their evil, I will repent of the evil that I thought to do unto them." Jeremiah 18:8 KJV

In the above verse, the King James Bible has God *repenting* of evil. Contrast the New King James, which states: "I will relent of the disaster that I thought to bring upon them."

Copyright 2005 Edward G. Palmer, All Rights Reserved.

Book of Edward—Chapter 6

The Heart of an Apostle

> "If it do evil in MY sight, that it obey not MY voice, then I will repent of the good, wherewith I said I would benefit them." Jeremiah 18:10 KJV

In the above verse, the King James Bible has God actually *repenting* of doing good. Contrast the New King James, which states: "I will relent concerning the good with which I said I would benefit it."

> "If so be they will hearken, and turn every man from his evil way, that I may repent ME of the evil, which I purpose to do unto them because of the evil of their doings."
> Jeremiah 26:3 KJV

In the above verse, the King James Bible has God *repenting* of evil. Contrast the New King James, which states: "That I may relent concerning the calamity which I purpose to bring on them because of the evil of their ways."

> "Therefore now amend your ways and your doings, and obey the voice of the LORD your God; and the LORD will repent HIM of the evil that HE hath pronounced against you."
> Jeremiah 26:13 KJV

In the above verse, the King James Bible has God *repenting* of evil. Contrast the New King James, which states: "Then the LORD will relent concerning the doom that HE has pronounced against you."

> "If ye will still abide in this land, then will I build you, and not pull you down, and I will plant you, and not pluck you up: for I repent ME of the evil that I have done unto you."
> Jeremiah 42:10 KJV

In the above verse, the King James Bible has God *repenting* of evil. Contrast the New King James, which states: "For I relent concerning the disaster that I have brought upon you."

The Heart of an Apostle

> "I the LORD have spoken it: it shall come to pass, and I will do it; I will not go back, neither will I spare, neither will I repent; according to thy ways, and according to thy doings, shall they judge thee, saith the LORD God."
>
> **Ezekiel 24:14 KJV**

Ezekiel again makes the case that what God has spoken will come to pass. The New King James Bible translates the KJV language of "neither will I *repent*" into "Nor will I relent."

> "Who can tell if God will turn and repent, and turn away from HIS fierce anger, that we perish not?" Jonah 3:9 KJV

Who can tell? Indeed, if you have the heart of an apostle, you know that God does not have anything to *repent* to mankind for. HE is the potter. It is us who are the clay in HIS hands. The New King James translates the above verse as: "Who can tell if God will turn and relent?"

Finally, on the issue of infallibility in the King James Bible, you will find that the word "infallible" is used only once and it is in Acts 1:3.

> "To whom also he shewed himself alive after his passion by many infallible proofs, being seen of them forty days, and speaking of the things pertaining to the kingdom of God"
>
> **Acts 1:3 KJV**

> "To whom he also presented himself alive after his suffering by many infallible proofs, being seen by them during forty days and speaking of the things pertaining to the kingdom of God." Acts 1:3 NKJV

Note that the New King James maintains the use of the word infallible. That is an example of how close the NKJV is to the KJV. However, if you attempt to research the word "infallible" back to its original Hebrew or Greek using Strong'S, you will find that there is no root.

The Heart of an Apostle

When there is no Hebrew or Greek root word cited, it only means that the translators have "added" the word into play. It could be an excellent word based on the resources the translators had available; but you need to understand that it was chosen vs. actually being a part of an original Hebrew or Greek manuscript. Other translations use a phrase like "convincing evidence" in Acts 1:3. Yes, God inspired the Holy Bible. However, it is not infallible [inerrant] and the above verses should suffice to make that point to you. I might note that God continues to this day to inspire writers.

Your ability to discern whether or not a writer is actually inspired by God instead of Satan is simple. Does Holy Scripture back the writer's thoughts? In other words, can the writer help you connect the dots between different Scripture so you can SEE THE TRUTH OF SCRIPTURE FOR YOURSELF? Or, do you need to take a leap of faith to accept the writer's points? If the Scriptures do not speak for themselves as presented by the writer [speaker, teacher or apostle], it is a sign that they ARE NOT OF GOD.

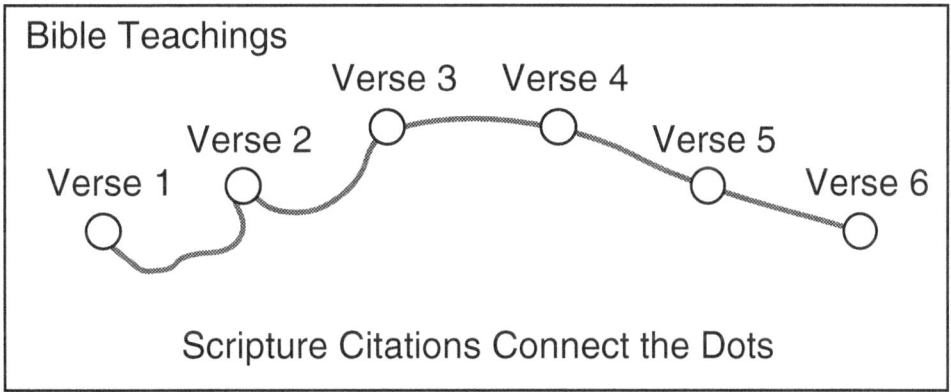

In the above illustration, a teacher [etc.] walks you through various Scriptures needed to illustrate a spiritual principle to you. Scriptures speak for themselves in full support of the discussion and main points that the speaker is trying to get across. For example, in the cited Scriptures on King James, did you have to take my word for it that the King James Bible is errant? Or, can you see for yourself from the Scriptures I cited? Note: It is up to you to check all Scripture citations. One of Satan's tricks is to quote non-existent Bible verses to an ignorant congregation either lacking Bibles or the conviction "to test the spirit" for truth [look up the citation].

The Heart of an Apostle

An even more subtle way that Satan deceives believers is to simply "misquote" Scripture ever so slightly. Off just enough to make it convincing to you that Scripture itself connects the dots. However, unwittingly, you wind up accepting lies instead of God's truth. Do not accept misquoted Bible Scripture from any teacher. Once you realize the speaker is inserting error or his own opinion into Scripture, you need to confront them and get out. If you have the heart of an apostle, you will not tolerate apostasy in any form from those who profess they know God's Word.

Many churches have congregations that do not even carry a Bible. While some churches have Bibles located under the pews, the message is clear that you do not have to read the Bible to attend "our congregation." I tell you that if you do not read the Bible, you can never know God's truth and whether you are in God's house or Satan's house. Many churches are nothing less than elaborate and deceptive dens of Satan. If you are ignorant of the Holy Bible, how will you tell which house you are actually in? If you call yourself a believer in Christ, do you not also see a responsibility to the word of God?

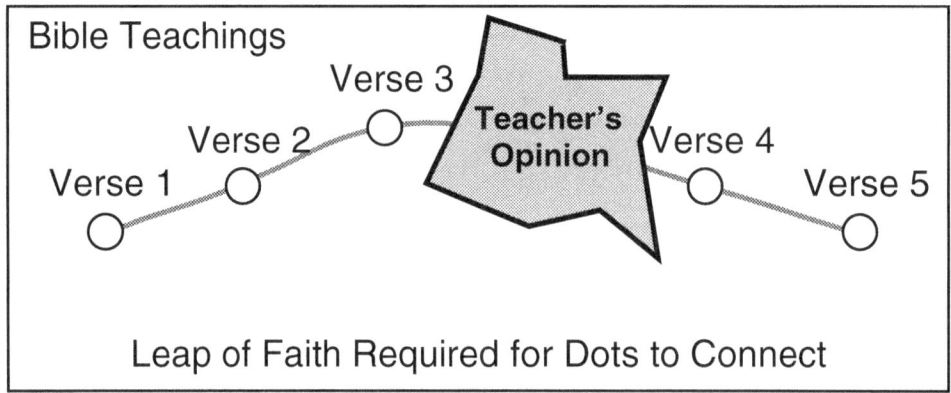

In the above illustration Scripture citations do not connect to one another to support the Bible teaching. Instead, you need to take a leap of faith from one Scripture to the next. Often, this leap of faith, is taking the teacher at his or her opinion. Sometimes it is accepting errant Scripture that you know does not line up with your Bible. This is the work of Satan in the church today. The teachings are designed to take you off God's truth.

The Heart of an Apostle

While the debate over which Bible translation is the best rages on, it important to realize that they are all prone to similar types of errors as shown above in the King James. Some have curious quirks to them. Some have suspicious things about them. Still, all do seem to agree on the important principles of God. Curiously, despite this general agreement and the fact that the translations are pretty much 99% error free, various doctrines exist today in Christianity that do, actually contradict established biblical text.

> **If you have the heart of an apostle, the truth of God's Holy Word is more important to you than the translation [or book, teacher or apostle] from which it came.**

Yes, God's truth is also more important than the notion of being 100% perfect on our own or having, in our possession, an inerrant Bible. Having learned Satan's tricks for taking you off course with biblical instruction inside the church, what else can you do? What also keeps you smart enough to discern God's truth? It is simply "abiding in HIS Word."

> **"Then said Jesus to those Jews which believed on him, if ye continue in my word, then are ye my disciples indeed; [32] and ye shall know the truth, and the truth shall make you free." John 8:31-32 KJV**

The New King James states: *"If you abide in my word."* The message is simply that God's Word is the truth for our life here on planet earth and our ability or lack of ability to discern truth is directly connected to our knowledge of the Bible and whether or not we "abide in it [the Bible]." Secondly, as your walk with God grows strong, HIS Spirit will set all things straight for you in accordance with what the Apostle John taught us.

> **"But the anointing which ye have received of him abideth in you, and ye need not that any man teach you: but as the same anointing teacheth you of all things, and is truth, and is no lie, and even as it hath taught you, ye shall abide in him." 1 John 2:27 KJV**

The Heart of an Apostle

Those with a heart of an apostle understand they need to stay strong in God's Holy Word. By abiding in the word of God, you will find yourself in fellowship with God daily. You may even talk to HIM all the waking hours of your life. When Paul said to "pray without ceasing" in 1 Thess 5:17, he was telling us that we can fellowship with God throughout our day. I certainly do and I cannot tell you the amount of joy it has brought into my life. You can find yourself being physically directed by the Holy Spirit just as the Spirit directs the fingers of my hands while I type. The combination of Bible knowledge and the Spirit's help inside of us will provide you with strong discernment. Then, be humble and willing to go do your homework when it is needed.

Finally, on sin, Timothy provides the following instructions.

"But God's truth stands firm like a great rock, and nothing can shake it. It is a foundation stone with these words written on it: 'The LORD knows those who are really HIS, and a person who calls himself a Christian should not be doing things that are wrong.'" 2 Tim. 2:19 LIV

And James provides the following definition on SIN.

"So any person who knows what is right to do but does not do it, to him it is sin." James 4:17 AMP

The above two citations illustrate the language of other modern English translations. However, the verses cited have the same meaning in all the other Bibles I use. Note that the clear message from Timothy is that we are not to do wrong. Note also that James makes it clear that when we do wrong we sin. Do you remember the words of Jesus to "sin no more?"

I have come to rather appreciate James 4:17 and I now view it as a catch all for mankind's sin. You see, what is right or wrong depends upon each individual's perspective and knowledge. God will hold me to a much higher standard because of my knowledge of the Bible and the resources I have to ferret out HIS truth—over that of a new believer.

The Heart of an Apostle

My education and experience may suggest a different right course of action over another person just because I may see things differently. I may see an event larger or smaller than another person. I may see it in a different context altogether because of my background. Still, there are always the right and wrong things to do for all of us in any situation, even for you.

The most fascinating and overlooked aspect of James 4:17 comes from the idea that all of us will be held accountable for sin every time we do something wrong. Regardless of what our knowledge is about God's Word or any other given subject, there will always be that right and wrong thing to do for everyone. Perhaps even a list of right and wrongs things that can be done in a given circumstance. No matter who you are and what level of education or experience you have, God's spirit is the thing inside of you that always tells you what is right and what is wrong. HE will separate out the things on your list for you, if you will listen to HIM.

When You Don't Do The Right Thing, God Calls It Sin!

James 4:17 is the best definition of sin you will find. Your knowledge of the Bible should be good enough to not buy into the nonsense that the Ten Commandments no longer apply to your life. It should also be good enough so you do not dismiss [ignore] the words of Jesus.

Was Jesus Christ an apostle of God [messenger from God] or was he actually God manifested in the flesh, as so many Christians believe today? Is it possible to be both? If so, how? The answers to these questions are at the heart of the Christian trinity question. And, they are in this book.

Today's Dictionary of the Bible[1], Guideposts Edition — *1982 Bethany House Publishers* defines the word "apostle" as follows:

Apostle *A person sent by another; a messenger; envoy.* This word is used as a descriptive designation of Jesus Christ, the Sent of the FATHER (John 20:21; Hebrews 3:1)

The Heart of an Apostle

Jesus Christ Was An Apostle of God!

"Then said Jesus to them again, 'Peace be unto you: as my FATHER hath sent me, even so send I you.' " John 20:21 KJV

"Wherefore, holy brethren, partakers of the heavenly calling, consider the *apostle* and High Priest of our profession, Christ Jesus." Hebrews 3:1 KJV

The Bible makes it perfectly clear that Jesus was a messenger [apostle] from God Almighty. When you have the heart of an apostle, you seek to understand Jesus. You do not ignore nor dismiss his words. Now, please note that it is the words of Jesus in John 20:21. Does this matter?

The respected New Strong'S Exhaustive Concordance of the Bible[2] *1990 Thomas Nelson Publishers* defines the word "apostle" as follows:

Apostle   Men divinely commissioned to represent Christ.

The American Heritage Dictionary[3] defines the word "apostle" as:

Apostle   1. One of a group made up esp. of the 12 disciples chosen by Christ to preach his gospel. 2. A missionary of the early Christian Church. 3. A leader of the first Christian mission to a country or region. 4. One of the 12 members of the Mormon administrative council. 5. One who leads or advocates a cause or movement.

Who are those listed in the Bible as Apostles? If you have any knowledge of the Bible, you know that there were not just twelve apostles. But, did you realize that Jesus Christ himself was an apostle of God? Do you understand the message that God gave Jesus to tell us?

The Heart of an Apostle

Ninety-Six Apostles Identified

No.	Name of Apostle	Bible Reference
1	Jesus Christ [the head and chief apostle]	Hebrews 3:1
2	Simon [who is called Peter]	Matthew 10:2
3	Andrew [the brother of Simon]	Matthew 10:2
4	James [the son of Zebedee]	Matthew 10:2
5	John [brother of James & son of Zebedee]	Matthew 10:2
6	Philip	Matthew 10:3
7	Bartholomew	Matthew 10:3
8	Thomas	Matthew 10:3
9	Matthew [the tax collector]	Matthew 10:3
10	James [son of Alphaeus]	Matthew 10:3
11	Lebbaeus [whose surname was Thaddaeus]	Matthew 10:3
12	Simon [the Cananite]	Matthew 10:4
13	Judas Iscariot	Matthew 10:4
14	Matthias	Acts 1:26
15	Barnabas	Acts 13:2
16	Paul	Acts 13:2
17	James [the brother of Jesus Christ]	Galatians 1:19
18	Silvanous	1 Thess 1:1
19	Timothy	1 Thess 1:1
20	Andronicus	Romans 16:7
21	Junias	Romans 16:7
22	Apollos	1 Corinthians 3:22
23	Cephas	1 Corinthians 3:22
24	Luke	2 Timothy 4:11
25	Titus	Titus 1:4
26	Jude	Jude 1:1
27-96	The "other seventy" appointed by Christ	Luke 10:1

With very little effort and nothing more than Strong'S concordance and a KJV Bible, you can come up with the above list of 96 apostles. You might ask, did Christ stop with these apostles or did he appoint others?

Copyright 2005 Edward G. Palmer, All Rights Reserved.

Book of Edward—Chapter 6

The Heart of an Apostle

> "After these things the Lord appointed other seventy also, and sent them two and two before his face into every city and place, whither he himself would come." **Luke 10:1 KJV**
>
> "And HE HIMSELF gave some to be apostles, some prophets, some evangelists, and some pastors and teachers."
> **Ephesians 4:11 NKJV**

God has never stopped appointing apostles and others to do HIS work here on earth and that much is very clear. So, exactly what do apostles do for God? Is it God they serve or Christ they serve? Do apostles make a distinction between God and Christ? If so, why? Aren't they the same?

Again, using Strong'S® Concordance and a KJV Bible, we can come up with the following list of things that apostles do for God.

No.	Description of Task or Mission	Bible Reference
1	Perform Miracles	Matthew 10:1,8
2	Preach the Gospel	Matthew 28:19-20
3	Witness for Resurrection	Acts 1:22
4	Write Scripture	Ephesians 3:5
5	Establish the Church	Ephesians 2:19-20
6	Interpret Prophecy	Acts 2:14-36
7	Defend Truth	Phil. 1:7, 17
8	Expose Heretics	Galatians 1:6-9
9	Uphold Discipline	2 Cor. 13:1-6
10	Establish Churches	Romans 15:17-20
11	Deliver a Message to Jews	Matthew 15:24; Acts 20:21
12	Deliver a Message to Gentiles	Acts 15:7; 2 Timothy 4:17

The most fundamental and basic task of an apostle is to deliver a message for God. Secondly, and no less important, is to deliver the message that God gave Jesus Christ to deliver. Christ's message was the same as all the earlier ones from God concerning salvation: "Repent and be saved."

The Heart of an Apostle

Did God's message on salvation to mankind ever change? No, it didn't. From time immemorial the salvation message is fundamentally the same. When Christ started preaching, he said: "Repent for the kingdom of Heaven is at hand." [Matthew 4:17] Today, the message I write is the same, with some added emphasis directed at those who call themselves Christian. However, this is the same basic message from God. It is "repentance [first] and salvation [second]," exactly in that order.

I was waiting for the first question to arrive concerning the audacity to call myself an apostle. After all, aren't there only 12 apostles in totality? This is a common ignorance in the church at large. How can there be another one rising up in the twenty-first century? It was a predictable question from a Christian more concerned about authority than God's Holy Word.

So Edward, "Exactly who appointed you an apostle?"

My answer is the same as Paul's. I serve God first and Christ second. Like Paul, my apostleship is "not of men, neither by man, but by Jesus Christ, and of God the FATHER."

The message I received from God: Is to explain to Christians why many, if not a majority, will be going to Hell instead of Heaven. I write nothing new! Instead, as God has commanded of me, I remind you, who claim to be the salt of the earth, the words God has already provided. HIS message has always been the same one to mankind. **REPENT and BE SAVED!**

The next question came from the heart of a sincere believer, a seeker of truth, who gently asked: "Ed, do you really consider yourself to be an apostle?" I responded: "This is something that I struggled with for many years. I also ignored God's call for over two years. If an apostle is someone with a message from God, then yes, I am indeed an apostle. For surely God has given me a message to deliver to all of Christianity." I might add that God's Spirit has been relentless on me for many years to get HIS message out. When this book is done, I will have completed God's main task.

The Heart of an Apostle

In Hebrews 3:1 we read to: "Consider the *apostle* and High Priest of our profession, Christ Jesus." As the message God has given me unfolds, you may start to ask yourself this important question: "Do you worship God or do you worship the Apostle Christ Jesus?" How about the High Priest Christ Jesus? Do you worship him? Would you consider any priest or apostle worthy of your worship? If so, why then is it clearly written to only worship God Almighty? Consider these words of Jesus Christ.

> **"Then saith Jesus unto him, get thee hence, Satan: for it is written, thou shalt worship the LORD thy God, and HIM only shalt thou serve." Matthew 4:10 KJV**
>
> **Jesus also said: "But the hour cometh, and now is, when the true worshippers shall worship the FATHER in spirit and in truth: for the FATHER seeketh such to worship HIM. God is a Spirit: and they that worship HIM must worship HIM in spirit and in truth." John 4:23-24 KJV**

When you have the heart of an apostle, it is God the FATHER that you worship. You recognize that Jesus Christ is the head apostle and the leader of our worship service as the High Priest in the temple of our God. You don't worship Jesus Christ per se, but you honor him in all you do. Every time you pray to the FATHER in Christ's name, you honor Jesus Christ. You also work with Jesus Christ to serve the ONE true God in a hierarchy of service that God established. Jesus calls God the "FATHER." God also calls us into the continued work of Jesus Christ in getting God's message out.

For millennium, mankind has not listened to the words of Jesus. Let me remind you that the Bible states clearly who Jesus is. It states Jesus is an apostle of God. That he goes back to Heaven to serve God as our High Priest. Yet, many Christians worship Jesus instead of God. They are confused by a trinity doctrine that cannot be reconciled with the written word of God. Do you seek the truth? If you are the type that does not seek the truth, you might as well close of this book right now. It is too late for you. God has written off everyone who is not a "lover of the truth."

The Heart of an Apostle

As I write, I will quote from God's Word. You, yourself, will have to decide if you will OBEY what God has already provided to you in simple sixth grade language that all can understand. If you want to judge my apostleship, then judge the totality of this book and its conformance to the written word of God.

Today, I would die upside down on a cross before forsaking my God. For that matter, I would die upside down on a cross before forsaking my brother Jesus Christ. Yes, Jesus Christ is NOT my God. He is my brother and he is a brother to all who do God's will. Like Paul, Christ is "my hope in whom I live for God." [1 Timothy 1:1] Think about Apostle Paul's words.

The denial of the words of Christ by the truth squad at Thursday night's Bible study was the final straw for me. That is when I stood up and looked at the young men and told them:

> **"I will tell you something that only an apostle will tell you. If you refuse to accept the words of Christ, you do not belong to God and HIS Spirit is not inside of you." Edward**

I tell you the same thing. You cannot dismiss or otherwise explain away the words of Jesus Christ simply because it inconveniently contradicts your Christian theology. Why? It's because Jesus represented God in everything he said and did. It was not God in the flesh in the likeness of Jesus; it was God using HIS human begotten Son Jesus as HIS spokesperson.

> **"Then said Jesus unto them, when ye have lifted up the Son of man, then shall ye know that I am he, and that I do nothing of myself; but as my FATHER hath taught me, I speak these things." John 8:28 KJV**

> **"I must work the works of HIM that sent me, while it is day: the night cometh, when no man can work." John 9:4 KJV**

Jesus spoke for God and did only what God told him to do.

The Heart of an Apostle

If you want to believe that God came down in the flesh and died on the cross, then you must also believe that God committed suicide on the cross. That would have to be your intellectually honest conclusion. After all, no one can kill the omnipotent awesome God who created us. If you believe that HE committed suicide, you will then have to conclude that HE had to repent for something. Why else would God commit suicide? Such is the nonsense of today's Christianity. If you stick around, this is a subject I will talk further on in a later chapter. It was not God on the cross. It was Jesus Christ, the only begotten human Son of God on the cross!

"Who is he that overcometh the world, but he that believeth that Jesus is the Son of God?" 1 John 5:4 KJV

"But who could possibly fight and win this battle except by believing that Jesus is truly the Son of God?"
1 John 5:5 Living

The Bible makes it clear that those who actually overcome the world and win the battle for salvation really believe that Jesus is the Son of God. The Holy Bible does not state we should believe that Jesus was God; make a note of it. That's why the Bible does not state or imply anywhere that God repented on the cross committing suicide. Think about the plain and simple words of the Apostle John above. Then think about the implications of the God on the cross theology and why it doesn't measure up to biblical text.

When you have the heart of an apostle, the words of all the books of the Bible are important to you. You understand that, collectively, they represent a beautiful mosaic created for your human benefit while on earth. Created to enhance your joy and ensure your eternal life in Heaven after this short earthly existence. You know the books are interwoven and presented as a whole, a complete work of God. When you have the heart of an apostle, you don't try to then take God's Word out of context. This could be either the biblical context or the context of the character of God Almighty. You also do not try to parse sentences to create your own doctrine.

The Heart of an Apostle

Once again "consider" the words of Jesus as he describes two different methods and sets of criteria for you to enter into eternal life.

> **So he said to him, "Why do you call me good? No one is good but ONE, that is, God. But if you want to enter into life, keep the commandments." He said to him [Jesus], "Which ones?" Jesus said, "You shall not murder, you shall not commit adultery, you shall not steal, you shall not bear false witness, honor your father and your mother, and, you shall love your neighbor as yourself." The young man said to him [Jesus], "All these things I have kept from my youth." Matthew 19:17-20 NKJV**

For Eternal Life, Obey God's Commandments!

> **"And behold, a certain lawyer stood up and tested him, saying, 'Teacher, what shall I do to inherit eternal life?' He [Jesus] said to him, 'What is written in the law? What is your reading of it?' So he answered and said, 'You shall love the LORD your God with all your heart, with all your soul, with all your strength, and with all your mind, and your neighbor as yourself.' And he [Jesus] said to him [the lawyer], 'You have answered rightly; do this and you will live.'" Luke 10:25-28 NKJV**

For Eternal Life, Love God With All Your Heart!

Was Jesus lying when he provided the above two instructions for entering into eternal life? Do you dismiss or ignore these words of Christ? If so, do you also ignore the words of Christ that state he only spoke what God Almighty [his FATHER] told him to say? These are not Christ's criteria; they are God's!

This is not the last discussion on the issue of the trinity doctrine. I will return to the subject and cover it in more depth during a later chapter. For now, God poses a simple question to you. Do you *really* accept Christ?

If you accept the salvation of Christ, do you also understand the ramifications of the salvation criteria that Christ provided? Many Christians think they have a free lunch with God. That they can simply mouth that Jesus is their Lord and then be assured once and for all of eternal life. God has called me to explain to you why this is not how salvation works.

How did we get to this state of confusion with the simple and plain words written in the Bible? To the point where organized Christianity would preach apostasy from the pulpits in direct contradiction to the word of God? When I asked God that question, he gave me the answer and an experience of suffering through rationalization for four days until I fully understood HIS answer. The short version is that "there is no limit to the rationalization of man." God told me that in order to intellectually support mankind's trinity, diverse theologies were developed. The centerpiece of all those theologies is that they summarily dismiss the written word of God.

The truth squad never realized that God had brought an apostle to listen in at last Thursday's Bible Study. God placed me there to show me how deep the apostasy had grown in Christianity. It has grown so deep, that these four young men, like a lot of those in Christianity, simply dismiss or ignore the words of the very savior they claim to embrace.

"When you have the heart of an apostle, you study carefully what Jesus taught and you obey him. It's because Christ was more than a willing sacrifice, he was a teacher of God's truth!" The Apostle Edward

When You Give God Your Heart, It Can Grow Into …
The Heart of an Apostle

Book of Edward

Chapter Seven
Choices From The Heart

— Deuteronomy 30:19 —

"I call Heaven and earth as witnesses today against you, that I have set before you life and death, blessing and cursing; therefore choose life, that both you and your descendants may live." NKJV

"I call Heaven and earth to record this day against you, that I have set before you life and death, blessing and cursing: therefore choose life, that both thou and thy seed may live." KJV

"I call Heaven and earth to witness against you that today I have set before you life or death, blessing or curse. Oh, that you would choose life; that you and your children might live!" LIV

"This day I call Heaven and earth as witnesses against you that I have set before you life and death, blessings and curses. Now choose life, so that you and your children may live." NIV

"Today, I call Heaven and earth to witness against you: I am offering you life or death, blessing or curse. Choose life, then, so that you and your descendants may live." NJB

"I call Heaven and earth to witness against you today that I have set before you life and death, blessings and curses. Choose life so that you and your descendants may live." NRSV

"I call on Heaven and earth as witnesses today that I have offered you life or death, blessings or curses. Choose life so that you and your descendants will live." GW

Choices From The Heart

Your new life walking with God started at the very moment you gave God your heart. It was a huge CHOICE that you made directly from your heart. This should have been a point of total surrender to God's authority that you eventually came to in life. You may have reached that decision of your heart either through a great struggle or tragedy in your life or through simply a gift of understanding that God gave you. For me, personally, it was through the gift of understanding that God gave me on one particular day after 32 years of wandering around spiritually in life. Admittedly, it was a low point in my life and my heart was fully open to His Spirit. It was an epiphany that I will never forget.

If you have not reached the point of total [100%] surrender to God, it is unlikely that you are truly walking with God. You may, instead, possess a certain amount of head knowledge of God that hasn't moved down to your heart. God has instructed us through the teachings of Jesus that: "You will know them by their fruits." This "knowing them" would also include the choices you make in life. The choices we make in life are precursors to the blessings or cursings we receive in life. Choices are themselves a fruit.

Those who walk with God are slaves unto righteousness and make choices FOR GOD throughout each day. They also live in the present moment understanding the teachings of Jesus that we are not meant to live with worries about tomorrow, next week, month, year, etc. Do you get the picture on not worrying that Jesus provided for us? Each day is comprised of righteous choices for God. A righteous day leads to righteous weeks, which leads to righteous months, years and a lifetime of service to God.

For now, I will assume that since you call yourself a Christian, that you have made a choice from the heart that is a 100% surrender to God. If so, it means you have chosen life and blessings over death and curses as God has asked us to do. You have made the first choice of the rest of your life.

Choose Life & Blessings Over Death & Curses!

For purposes of illustrating how much the various Bible translations actually agree, God instructed me to show you the above seven translations of Deuteronomy 30:19.

Choices From The Heart

I could, however, have provided a lengthy list of 20 or more Bible translations and you would find that they are all in agreement on this subject matter. With few exceptions, all the Bible translations are in agreement and I will state that I believe this to be on 99% of the text. Excluding some nuances as illustrated in the last chapter, you can trust in your Bible. When you walk with God, HIS Spirit will also sort out and correct these nuances.

But Edward, you say: "Give me a break. You are quoting from the Old Testament. Isn't it true that the Old Testament no longer matters?" You are certainly right about the Old Testament citation. However, if you have a heart for God, you understand that God has not changed as a result of Jesus. That is truly the stuff of Christian mythology. Consider the following verse from the book of the Prophet Malachi in which God speaks for HIMSELF.

> **"For I am the LORD, I do not change!" Malachi 3:6**

This verse in Malachi is not a quotation from the Lord Jesus Christ; it is a quotation directly from God Almighty. If God has not changed, you need to listen to what God says. Our Bible teaches us in Hebrews 13:8 that: "Jesus Christ is the same yesterday, today, and forever." Therefore, you need to listen to Jesus as well.

I am constantly reminded of many preachers who teach that you can ignore the Old Testament and the Four Gospels. Their reasoning is that Paul provided you with a higher teaching from God; a teaching of "total freedom" through grace. Therefore, we should just live within the Epistles of Apostle Paul. However, the sheer arrogance of those preachers would have you ignore the Ten Commandments, the other words of God and the teachings of Christ that God provided. While it is true that certain aspects of the law have changed, I can tell you that you had better listen to the words of both God Almighty and HIS only begotten human Son, Jesus Christ.

Apostle Paul's words do not trump the words of God Almighty and Jesus Christ! If your preacher or teacher cannot explain Apostle Paul without ignoring the plain words of God Almighty and Jesus Christ, then they are teaching you apostasy. Listen to the words of Christ to the church at Ephesus in the Book of Revelation 2:6 "But this you have, that you hate

Choices From The Heart

the deeds of the Nicolaitans, which I also hate." God told Christ to compliment the church because they hated what the Nicolaitans were doing. In contrast, God told Christ to criticize the church at Pergamos for having Nicolaitans within their congregation [Rev 2:15].

Who "hated" the Nicolaitans? God Almighty and His Son Jesus Christ! Who were these Nicolaitans? Today's Dictionary of The Bible[1], *1982, Bethany House Publishers,* provides the following information:

Nicolaitans "The church at Ephesus (Rev. 2:6) is commended for hating the 'deeds' of the Nicolaitans, and the church of Pergamos is blamed for having them who hold their 'doctrines' (15). They were seemingly a class of professing Christians, who tried to introduce into the church a false freedom or licentiousness, thus abusing Paul's doctrine of grace (compare 2 Peter 2:15, 16, 19), and were probably identical with those who held the doctrine of Balaam (Rev. 2:14)."

Licentious "Pursuing desires aggressively and selfishly, unchecked by morality, especially in sexual matters." Microsoft Word 2001 Dictionary[2]

Listen to the words of Apostle Peter as he describes these types of people [the Nicolaitans who were licentious like Baalam] and then carefully consider the words of your own pastor or teacher.

"[14] Having eyes full of adultery and that cannot cease from sin, enticing unstable souls. They have a heart trained in covetous practices, and are accursed children. They have forsaken the right way and gone astray, following the way of Balaam the son of Beor, who loved the wages of unrighteousness; but he was rebuked for his iniquity: a dumb donkey speaking with a man's voice restrained the madness of the prophet. These are wells without water,

Choices From The Heart

> **clouds carried by a tempest, for whom is reserved the blackness of darkness forever. For when they speak great swelling words of emptiness, they allure through the lusts of the flesh, through lewdness, the ones who have actually escaped from those who live in error.**
>
> **[19] While they promise them liberty, they themselves are slaves of corruption; for by whom a person is overcome, by him also he is brought into bondage. For if, after they have escaped the pollutions of the world through the knowledge of the Lord and savior Jesus Christ, they are again entangled in them and overcome, the latter end is worse for them than the beginning. For it would have been better for them not to have known the way of righteousness, than having known it, to turn from the holy commandment delivered to them. But it has happened to them according to the true proverb: 'A dog returns to his own vomit,' and, 'a sow, having washed, to her wallowing in the mire.'"**
>
> 2 Peter 2:14-22

So your pastor [teacher] says you have "total freedom?" From whom or what do you have such freedom? Those who are free in Christ Jesus are "free indeed." Free to love God with 100% of their hearts and to do all that HE requires of them. Those free through Christ have their eyes on eternal life and not on <u>licentiousness</u> [sexual desires unchecked by morality] or on <u>lewdness</u> [an excessive preoccupation with sex that leads to lustful, obscene and indecent behavior] or on <u>lasciviousness</u> [sexually enticing behavior].

> **"Therefore if the Son makes you free, you shall be free indeed." John 8:36**

John makes it clear that "real believers" are free from sin. Phrased in another way, John means: "We are free from the control of our flesh and the sinful behavior that results from a lack of morality because the Spirit of God resides inside of us and we are no longer a captive of this world." One can't help but notice the descriptive words "A dog returns to his own vomit, and, a sow, having washed, to her wallowing in the mire." I am a witness for God

Copyright 2005 Edward G. Palmer, All Rights Reserved.

Choices From The Heart

to these times in which Christians do return to their lives of sin after having been first made free of those sins by Christ Jesus.

Peter aptly describes the strategy of the Nicolaitans who seek to destroy God's people and take them away from eternal life. These so-called Christians do not seek to openly say: "We are part of the devil's crowd and we would like you to join us." No, theirs is a work of deception and God's Word makes it clear that in the last days "a strong deception" will occur that threatens even the elect of God. The prophecy that began this book indicated that the people perished because they were not "lovers of the truth." Once again, the truth for your soul lies within the words of God and of HIS Son Jesus. If you cannot stomach reading the entire Bible, simply obtain a red letter Bible and read the words of Christ. For months, God told me: "It is all in the words of Jesus Christ, MY Son, as I gave Jesus to speak." Travel through the words of Christ and stay focused on those words and you will find eternal life. You will not find life in the teachings of the Nicolaitans [those who pervert of Paul's words]. You will only find death.

Now, I am certainly not here to tell you to obey the various laws on eating, sanitation, etc. However, you ignore those laws at your own risk. Likewise, you would not obey the laws on animal sacrifices for God. To do so makes a mockery of the sacrifice that Jesus Christ made on the cross.

So, I agree that the law has been modified somewhat with Christ. However, Jesus also "enhanced" the Ten Commandments with additional instructions [for our hearts] from God Almighty concerning murder, adultery and other subjects.

If you find yourself stuck in Paul's teachings and being advised to ignore the words of God Almighty [Ten Commandments, etc.] and the words of Jesus Christ [teachings on eternal life, righteousness, etc.], it is time to leave and leave fast. You are not in a congregation of God. You are in the modern congregation of the Nicolaitans whom God and Christ hate. You are among those whom Jesus will say: "I never knew you." In short, you have made a wrong choice from the heart. Change fellowships.

Copyright 2005 Edward G. Palmer, All Rights Reserved.

Book of Edward—Chapter 7

Choices From The Heart

Now let's go back to Deuteronomy 30:19 and see the entire context of God's instructions to HIS people to "choose." While this is directed at the Israelites, I tell you that you need to take these instructions to heart if you value your eternal life. I will use the words of the New Jerusalem Bible starting at Deuteronomy 30 verse 8 and ending at verse 20. Take heed.

"[8] And once again you will obey the voice of Yahweh your God and you will put all HIS commandments into practice, which I am laying down for you today. Yahweh your God will make you prosper in all your labours, in the offspring of your body, in the yield of your cattle and in the yield of your soil. For once again Yahweh will delight in your prosperity as HE used to take delight in the prosperity of your ancestors, if you obey the voice of Yahweh your God, by keeping HIS commandments and decrees written in the book of this Law, and if you return to Yahweh your God with all your heart and soul."

"[11] For this Law which I am laying down for you today is neither obscure for you nor beyond your reach. It is not in Heaven, so that you need to wonder, 'Who will go up to Heaven for us and bring it down to us, so that we can hear and practice it?' Nor is it beyond the seas, so that you need to wonder, 'Who will cross the seas for us and bring it back to us, so that we can hear and practice it?' No, the word is very near to you, it is in your mouth and in your heart for you to put into practice." *[In your heart to put into practice!]*

"[15] Look, today I am offering you life and prosperity, death and disaster. If you obey the commandments of Yahweh your God, which I am laying down for you today, if you love Yahweh your God and follow HIS ways, if you keep HIS commandments, HIS laws and HIS customs, you will live and grow numerous, and Yahweh your God will bless you in the country which you are about to enter and make your own. But if your heart turns away, if you refuse to listen, if you let yourself be drawn into worshipping other gods and

> serving them, I tell you today, you will most certainly perish; you will not live for long in the country which you are crossing the Jordan to enter and possess."
>
> "[19] Today, I call Heaven and earth to witness against you: I am offering you life or death, blessing or curse. Choose life, then, so that you and your descendants may live, in the love of Yahweh your God, obeying His voice, holding fast to Him; for in this your life consists, and on this depends the length of time that you stay in the country which Yahweh swore to your ancestors Abraham, Isaac and Jacob that He would give them." Deuteronomy 30:8-20 NJB

God's [Yahweh's] message was clear to His people thousands of years ago. Likewise, it is equally clear today. No matter how many teachers in Christianity tell you that your sin does not matter to God anymore, God's Word tells you differently. You <u>choose</u> whom you will serve!

> "And if it seems evil to you to serve the Lord, choose for yourselves this day whom you will serve, whether the gods which your fathers served that were on the other side of the river, or the gods of the Amorites, in whose land you dwell. But as for me and my house, we will serve the Lord."
> Joshua 24:15

"Choose For Yourself Whom You Will Serve!"

The <u>first</u> choice of your heart is to give it to God. The <u>second</u> choice of your heart is to obey God. The <u>third</u> choice of your heart is to obey Jesus Christ. The <u>fourth</u> choice of your heart is to fellowship in a house of God that honors ALL of God's Holy Word. The <u>fifth</u> choice of your heart is to not accept any teachings that discount, alter or dismiss any of the teachings of God or Jesus Christ. The <u>sixth</u> choice of your heart is to fellowship with friends who are also righteous. These choices move you closer to God and farther away from Satan. When you make righteous choices from your heart, you move closer to God. When you make sinful choices from your heart, you move closer to Satan.

Choices From The Heart

> **"The righteous should choose his friends carefully, for the way of the wicked leads them astray." Proverbs 12:26**

Each day we are faced with tens or even hundreds of choices. These choices are made either consciously or subconsciously [mental auto pilot]. Some are big choices with a dramatic impact on our earthly life. Some are small choices with a minor impact on our earthly life. Some of our choices have a spiritual element in them that impacts our future eternal life. Our choices can have a big impact in Heaven. Remember, when a sinner repents "there is joy in Heaven" [Luke 15:7]. While any particular sin may have little consequence on earth, it can have a huge impact in Heaven as nothing we do is hidden from God. Each choice we make in our life can be thought of as a crossroads in which we have the opportunity to move closer to God with our decision. Likewise, the wrong decision moves us away from God.

Your ability to make an informed decision for God is connected to your knowledge of the Bible and where your heart is with God. When you really love someone, you choose to make decisions that honor him or her. This is true of your spouse and it is true of God and His Son Jesus Christ. The graphic below is the basic choice diagram and its implications to move us closer to God or closer to Satan.

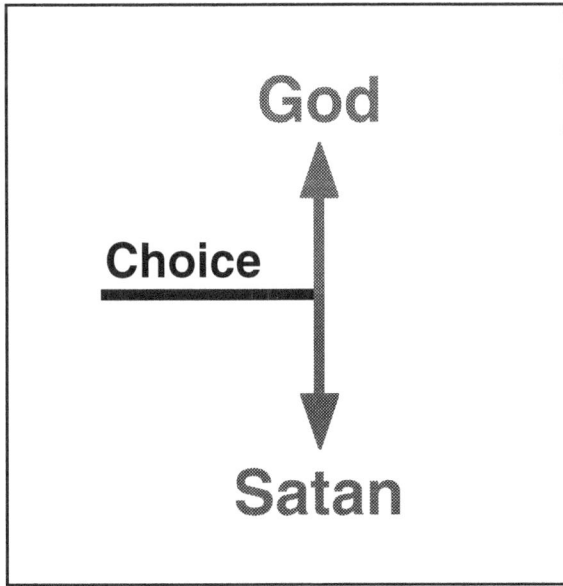

Our Choices Move Us Closer to God or Satan!

Choices From The Heart

The problem with the perverted grace doctrine of the Nicolaitans is that it ignores the two fundamental spiritual forces of God when it comes to choices. The fundamental forces are simple and straightforward and involve only two considerations. Those two considerations are righteousness and sin, which is the opposite of righteousness. Righteousness moves us closer to God and sin moves us closer to Satan. No matter what you might think of God's grace, it simply does not condone sin. Furthermore, Paul's teachings do not condone sin. To twist the Apostle Paul's grace teachings into the freedom to sin [licentiousness] is not only apostasy it is an utter abomination unto God. The two fundamental spiritual forces involving our choices can be viewed as shown in the graphic below.

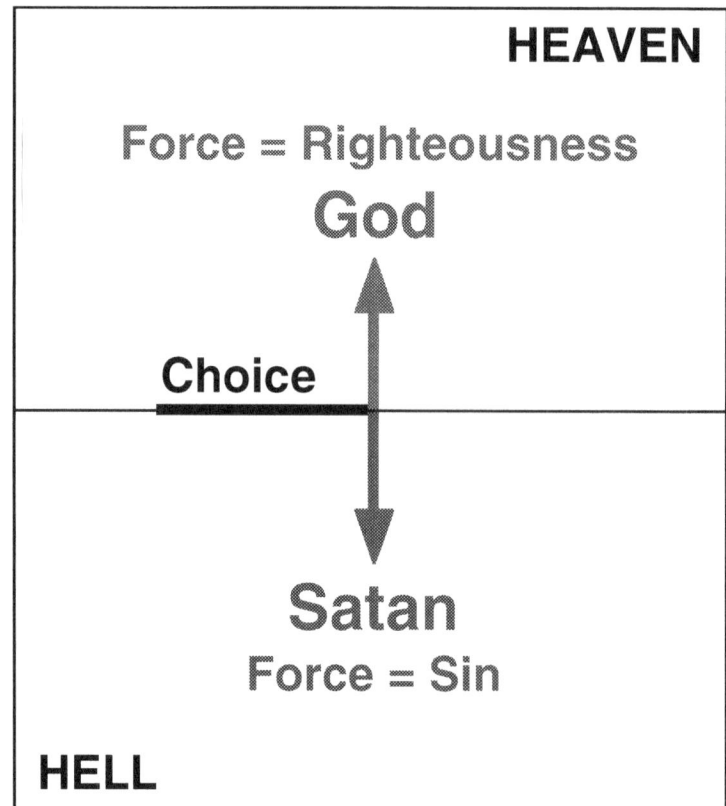

Our Choices Lead Us Into Heaven or Hell

Choices From The Heart

Life is really like the proverbial angel sitting on our "right" shoulder and whispering in our "right" ear to do good, while on the left shoulder the devil sits and whispers in that ear to do evil. Which voice do you listen to? While the metaphor seems trite in many respects, it is a very accurate depiction of the two very fundamental spiritual forces involved in each one of our choices. Good and evil, which is another way of saying righteousness and sin. When you engage in righteous choices, your spirit is edified [built up towards God]. When you engage in sinful choices, your spirit is defiled [corrupted and ruined, torn down towards Satan]. How else are you defiled?

Jesus said: "You are not defiled by what you eat; you are defiled by what you say and do!" Mark 7:15 NLT

Jesus said: "It is the thought-life that defiles you. For from within, out of a person's heart, come evil thoughts, sexual immorality, theft, murder, adultery, greed, wickedness, deceit, eagerness for lustful pleasure, envy, slander, pride, and foolishness. All these vile things come from within; they are what defile you and make you unacceptable to God." Mark 7:20-23 NLT

Note that Jesus clearly states <u>theft</u> is a vile thing that originates within a person's heart out of their evil thoughts. That a <u>theft</u> thought [and the others] defiles the person and makes them unacceptable to God. In chapter 16, when I explain the theft of Solid Rock Church, I will discuss why any pastor that steals a church will find no home with God. A pastor who steals a church from God, its denomination, and its congregation operates very deep on Satan's turf and has no fellowship with God. Such a pastor and all who support and work with him in the theft are key players on Satan's team working evil on this earth while pretending to be with God. Christians are not to steal [Eph 4:28] and the thief is excluded from Heaven [Matt. 6:20]. Those who steal churches are ignorant of the two basic spiritual forces in play on this earth, which I explained earlier. God is not real to their hearts.

Your Choices Either Edify Or Defile Your Life!

Copyright 2005 Edward G. Palmer, All Rights Reserved.

Book of Edward—Chapter 7

Choices From The Heart

> **So Jesus said, "Are you also still without understanding? Do you not yet understand that whatever enters the mouth goes into the stomach and is eliminated? But those things which proceed out of the mouth come from the heart, and they defile a man. For out of the heart proceed evil thoughts, murders, adulteries, fornications, thefts, false witness, blasphemies. These are the things which defile a man, but to eat with unwashed hands does not defile a man." Matthew 15:16-20 NKJV**

At any given moment [choice], we are either operating on God's turf or on Satan's turf. When we make a godly choice, we aim towards Heaven. When we engage in sin, we aim towards Hell. Apostle James reminds us in James 3:2 that we are all prone to stumble [sin]. Anyone who has ever taught others is aware of the propensity of the tongue to go wildly astray seemingly on its own accord. Only your heart can keep the tongue in check because that is where evil thoughts originate. The truth squad I talked about in the last chapter did not understand that fact in either Jesus' or in James' teachings. You will not be perfect; but you can certainly make righteous choices from your heart, especially if your heart walks with God Almighty.

> **"For we all stumble in many things. If anyone does not stumble in word, he is a perfect man, able also to bridle the whole body." James 3:2 NKJV**

> **"We all make many mistakes, but those who control their tongues can also control themselves in every other way."**
> **James 3:2 NLT**

Imagine for a moment that you are now in the process of making a choice. It doesn't matter what the choice is or whether it is big or small. Take a look back at the two preceding graphics. Your choice, whatever it is, will lead you in one of two separate and opposite directions. You will either move closer to God [going up] with a righteous choice or you will move closer to Satan [going down] with a choice to sin.

Choices From The Heart

That quiet inner voice you hear is God telling you what to do. To do what is righteous, you need to start listening to it [God]. IF that soft voice lines up with biblical teachings, this will be God's way of testifying to your spirit that it is indeed HE who speaks to you. IF that soft voice runs counter to the word of God, this will be God's way of testifying to your spirit that it is Satan whom you are listening to. Take heed. The truth is in God's Word.

Many Christians have never graduated into the basics of righteousness and ultimately this could pose a problem for their eternal life. The writer of Hebrews uses the metaphor of "babies on milk unskilled in righteousness."

> **"For though by this time you ought to be teachers, you need someone to teach you again the first principles of the oracles of God; and you have come to need milk and not solid food. [13] For everyone who partakes only of milk is unskilled in the word of righteousness, for he is a babe. [14] But solid food belongs to those who are of full age, that is, those who by reason of use have their senses exercised to discern both good and evil. [6:1] Therefore, leaving the discussion of the elementary principles of Christ, let us go on to perfection, not laying again the foundation of repentance from dead works and of faith toward God, [2] of the doctrine of baptisms, of laying on of hands, of resurrection of the dead, and of eternal judgment. [3] And this we will do if God permits. [4] For it is impossible for those who were once enlightened, and have tasted the heavenly gift, and have become partakers of the Holy Spirit, [5] and have tasted the good word of God and the powers of the age to come, [6] if they fall away, to renew them again to repentance, since they crucify again for themselves the Son of God, and put him to an open shame." Hebrews 5:12-6:6**

If you are unskilled in righteousness, you may not have graduated into the area of faith that places you above the minimum righteousness criteria that Jesus taught. You're not meant to live in sin. You are expected to graduate into righteousness.

Choices From The Heart

Once you understand each choice you make results in a directional movement towards either God or Satan, you will start to consciously ensure that the choices you make are righteous choices made from your heart. This is when you demonstrate spiritual maturity to God. You are *then* on your way to eternal life living on the level where you are a "partaker of the Holy Spirit 'tasting' the good word of God and the powers of the age to come."

WARNING. If you graduate to this level of spiritual maturity and you fall away [back to willful sin], it is *then impossible* to renew you once again to repentance. Why? It's because "you've crucified for yourself the Son of God and put him to an open shame." Rejection of righteousness at that level of spiritual maturity makes a mockery of Christ's sacrifice and disrespects God. Such people knew God intimately, but then blew HIM off! This issue does not apply to the typical backslider and those who worship and pray to Jesus Christ. Neither of these groups is intimate with God operating at that level of spiritual maturity. They can repent and rise to God's righteousness. However, the warning does apply to a lot of *evil* Christians in society.

You Need To Make Righteous Choices!

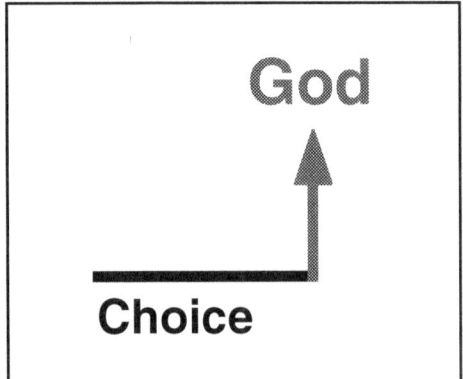

A Choice From The Heart For God

From an illustrative point of view, a choice from the heart for God is a decision to move up and closer to God. A pattern of choices for God looks like the graphic below. Likewise, a choice from the heart for Satan and a pattern of choices for Satan look like the two following graphics.

Choices From The Heart

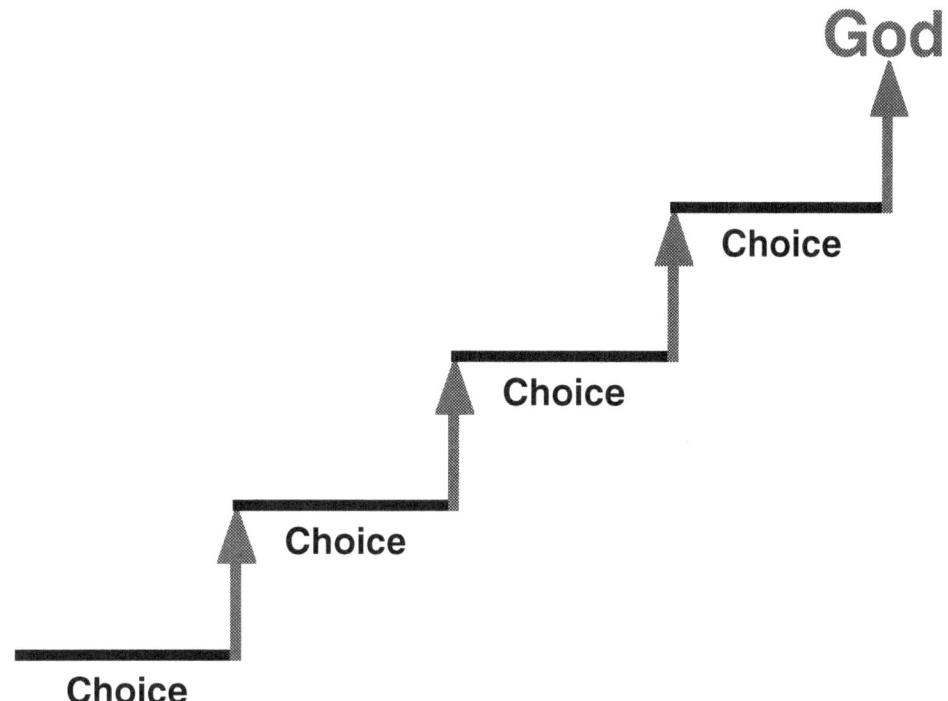

A Pattern Of Choices For God

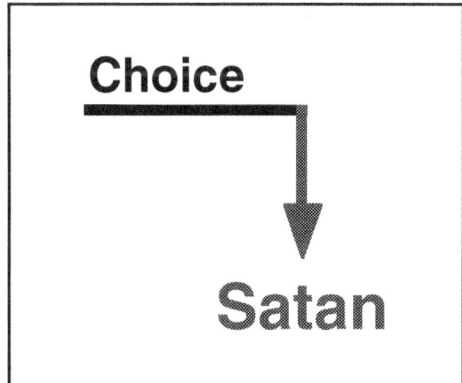

A Choice From The Heart For Satan

Choices From The Heart

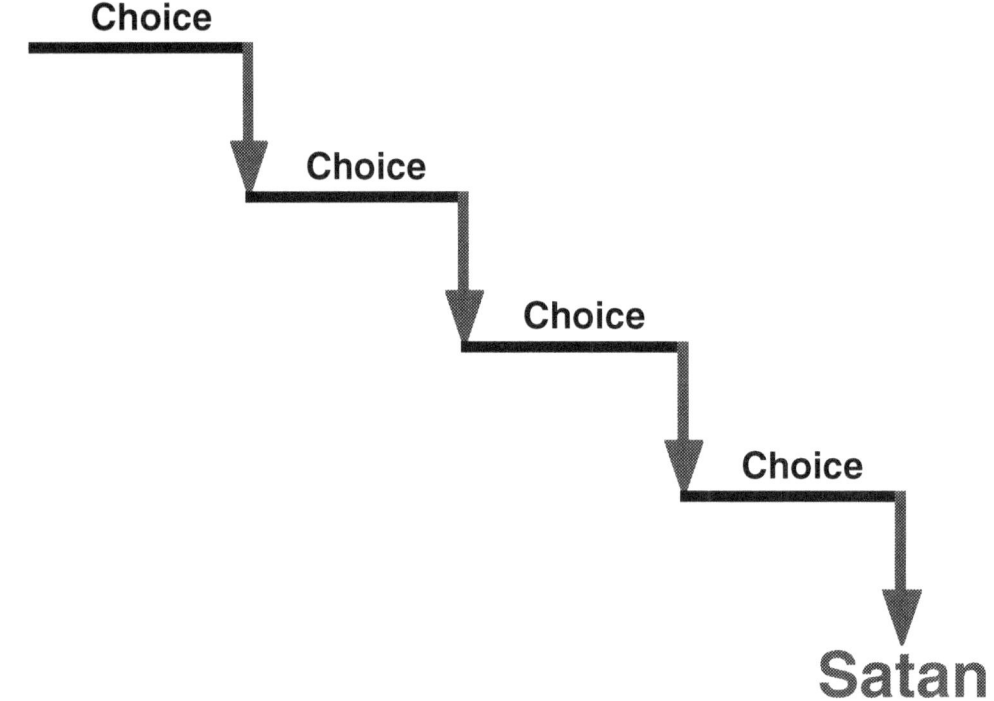

A Pattern Of Choices For Satan

Jesus makes it clear that our mouth is driven by what is in our heart and the evil thoughts that originates within it. Therefore, you need to make sure it is God's Spirit that resides in your heart along with the spirit of Christ. They will enable you to consistently make righteous choices from the heart.

> "At that day you will know that I am in my FATHER, and you in me, and I in you." John 14:20

> "I in them, and YOU in me; that they may be made perfect in ONE, and that the world may know that YOU have sent me, and have loved them as YOU have loved me."
> John 17:23

Choices From The Heart

If you are a real believer, God's Spirit resides inside of you and you listen to it. If you are a real believer in Jesus Christ, the spirit of Christ also resides inside of you and you listen to it. Ask yourself this question. If God and Christ were resident inside of your heart, would they help you make sinful choices from the heart? The answer is no. If you find it easy to make sinful choices from the heart, it is a sign that Satan's spirit is within you. You don't need to be an intellectual genius to figure this out.

At any given moment [of choice], you are not just going up towards God or down towards Satan. You are also simultaneously operating on either God's turf or Satan's turf. Therefore, you need to understand the two spiritual turfs we operate on as well as those two spiritual forces we have at our disposal to use as tools. The two turfs are shown in this graphic.

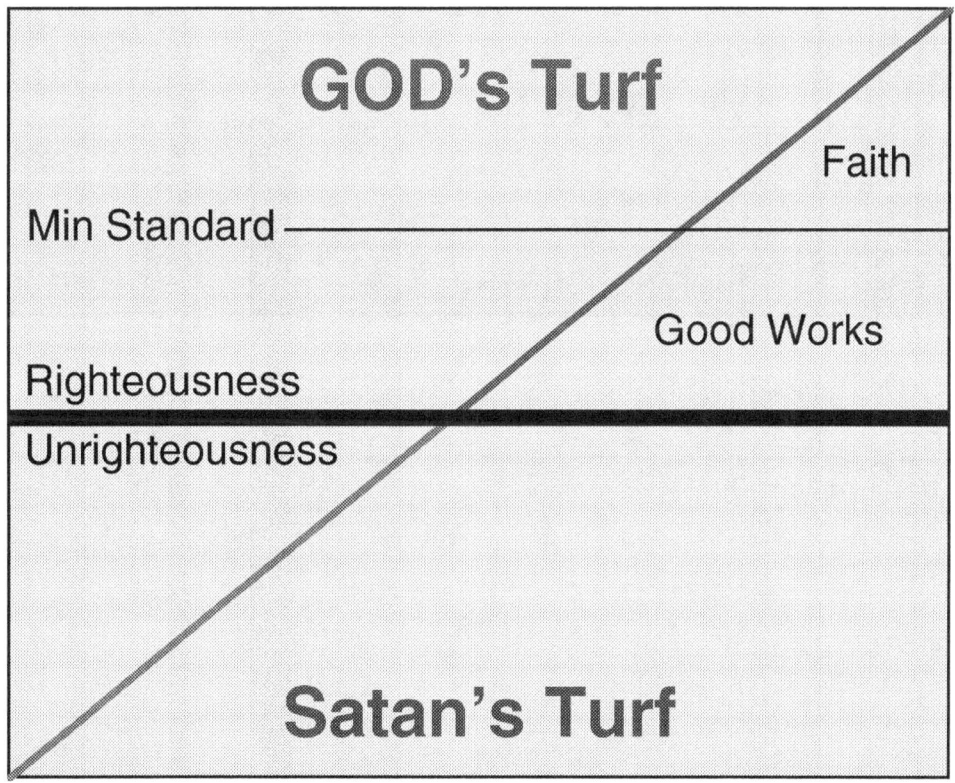

The Two Turfs Of Life

Choices From The Heart

148

While the above graphic shows both turfs combined, the graphic below shows God's turf and various degrees or percentages of righteousness. Remember that righteousness alone will not be good enough to enter eternal life unless it exceeds the minimum criteria set down by God. The good works of those whom Jesus told: "I never knew you" was evidence of this fact. When you exceed the minimum righteousness criteria, you walk with God in the area of faith and you are far away from sin. I will define the area of faith as the range between 51% and 99% righteousness; but only God knows the actual percentages. If God defined faith at the 80% or higher level in the illustration below, what would it mean in your life?

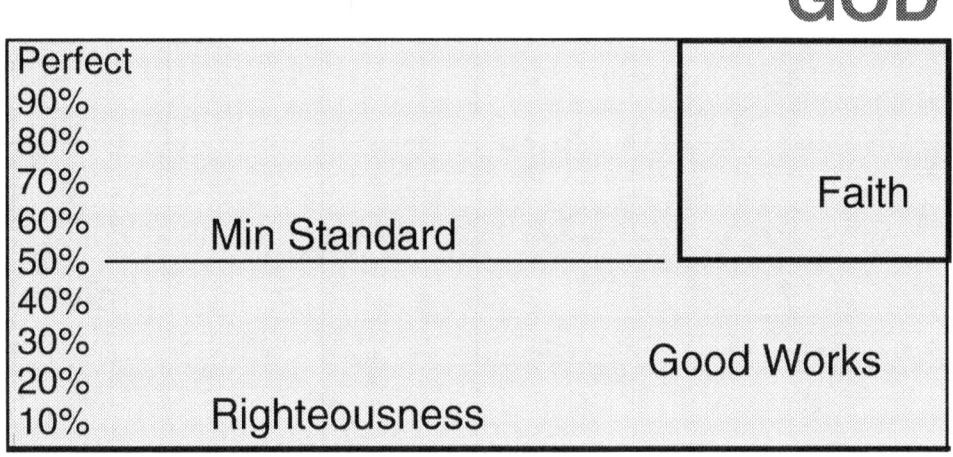

The second turf is illustrated below and it belongs to Satan.

10% Engaging in Sin, Evil, etc.	• Unrighteousness
20%	• Wickedness
30%	• Lawlessness
40%	• Iniquity
50%	• Disobedience
60%	• Evil
70%	• Sin
80%	
90% Stealing God's Property	

Satan

Copyright 2005 Edward G. Palmer, All Rights Reserved.

Book of Edward—Chapter 7

Choices From The Heart

Satan's turf is the area of unchecked morality and sin. One of Satan's big deceptions in Christianity today is a twisted doctrine on God's grace. The message is one of licentiousness by those who pervert Apostle Paul's teachings. It is a similar work of Baalam and the Nicolaitans. Yet, for God Almighty, the characteristics of those who operate on Satan's turf are clearly defined by characteristics of sin, evil, disobedience, iniquity, lawlessness, wickedness and unrighteousness. Anyone who knowingly does what is wrong commits sin in the eyes of God. Those who operate on Satan's turf at the level of stealing a church are down at the 90% unrighteousness level. They are very close to Satan and are active members of an evil team on this earth. Think your pastor is a righteous man? Does he pervert the word of God and preach man-made doctrines?

You need to be aware that from time immemorial, Satan has had his own ministers [and others] inside the church of God to deceive even those that are the elect of God. Are you a lover of the truth? If not, how will you know if you are being deceived by the very pastor who smiles at you and cordially greets you prior to and after your church gatherings? Paul makes it clear that Satan's ministers will appear under a false veil of righteousness. You need to look behind the smiles and greetings and into their teachings!

> **"Therefore it is no great thing if his [Satan's] ministers also transform themselves into ministers of righteousness, whose end will be according to their works." 2 Cor. 11:15**

> **"Who, knowing the righteous judgment of God, that those who practice such things are deserving of death, not only do the same but also approve of those who practice them."**
> **Romans 1:32**

> **"Do not judge according to appearance, but judge with righteous judgment." John 7:24**

Righteous Judgments Come From The Heart!

Copyright 2005 Edward G. Palmer, All Rights Reserved.

Choices From The Heart

> "For the eyes of the LORD are on the righteous, and HIS ears are open to their prayers; but the face of the LORD is against those who do evil." 1 Peter 3:12

> "If you know that he is righteous, you know that everyone who *practices* righteousness is born of HIM." 1 John 2:29

> "Little children, let no one deceive you. He who practices righteousness is righteous, just as he [Jesus] is righteous."
> 1 John 3:7

Practicing Righteousness Is A Choice Of The Heart!

The Bible makes it clear that there is a narrow path of life that leads to eternal life and a wide path of life that leads to destruction. We are told by Jesus to enter by the narrow gate.

> "Enter by the narrow gate; for wide is the gate and broad is the way that leads to destruction, and there are many who go in by it. Because narrow is the gate and difficult is the way which leads to life, and there are few who find it."
> Matthew 7:13-14

If you have not studied the words of Jesus in Matthew 7, this would be a good time to stop reading here and go to your Bible and check it out. After the admonishment to enter by the narrow gate, Jesus points out the deception, which will occur within the church. Jesus says: "Beware of the false prophets, who come to you in sheep's clothing [with angelic smiles and cordial greetings], but inwardly they are ravenous wolves. You will know them by their fruits."

I spent four years inside of a Christian cult. During those years, I always walked with God. While the pastor ranted his man made doctrines, I would study the Word. This pastor was clever to present himself as a righteous man of God. However, his teachings were off in very subtle ways.

Choices From The Heart

The pastor's appearance was angelic and his smile captivating. However, if anyone confronted him about apostasy, we never saw him or her again from that moment in time. The pastor expelled them from the church. By this method, he slowly eliminated the righteous of God out of the church. Today, it is left with only those ignorant of God's Word. Indeed, it is filled with those who travel the wide path, which leads to destruction [illustrated in the graphic below]. Please note that the wide path defined below contains 50% righteousness and 50% unrighteousness. The people who travel this path operate on both God's turf and Satan's turf. They believe that their sin makes no difference since they do good works. They never exceed the minimum righteousness requirement; they never operate in the area of faith in God.

GOD

God's People	Faith in God
God's Minimum Righteousness Standard	
Righteousness	Good Works
Unrighteousness	Evil Works
Satan's People	Faith in Satan

Satan

The Wide Path Leads To Destruction

Choices From The Heart

Yes, the pastor I am talking about was a perverter of God's Holy Word. He was, in essence, a modern day Nicolaitan and minister of Baalam. He preached righteousness, but practiced unrighteousness. The pastor fulfilled the words of Jesus in Matthew.

> **"Therefore whatever they tell you to observe, that observe and do, but do not do according to their works; for they say, and do not do. For they bind heavy burdens, hard to bear, and lay them on men's shoulders; but they themselves will not move them with one of their fingers."**
> **Matthew 23:3-4**

Getting your heart straight gets your mouth straight for God and reduces your stumbling. It also prevents you from being a perverter of God's Holy Word. When your heart and mouth are straight, you will NOT ignore the clear words of God Almighty and HIS only begotten Son Jesus Christ. You have the heart of an apostle and their words cannot be denied. You understand the truth concerning any man made alteration of the Word.

> **"Whatever I command you, be careful to observe it; you shall not add to it nor take away from it." Deut. 12:32**

> **"If anyone adds to these things, God will add to him the plagues that are written in this book; and if anyone takes away from the words of the book of this prophecy, God shall take away his part from the Book of Life, from the holy city, and from the things which are written in this book." Rev. 22:18-19**

Did God Almighty lie when HE said to "be careful to observe it?" That is the effect of a lot of Christian teachings today. God has not changed. The explanation for our collective ignorance in Christianity today lies in the area of our ignorance of God's Word and our collective unwillingness to obey. Rather than learn and become accountable to God, Christians walk the wide path to destruction content with the teachings of the Nicolaitans.

Choices From The Heart

Still, there is another path of life. It is the narrow way described by Jesus and it is shown in the graphic below. God's people understand that they "cannot [willfully] sin" as Apostle John has taught. They work aggressively to always be righteous people. They operate 100% above the minimum righteousness standard in the area of faith with God. They are far from sin and they reject sin in every choice they make. They reject the opportunity to sin regardless if anyone will know about it because they realize it cannot be hidden from God.

GOD

God's People	Faith in God
God's Minimum Righteousness Standard	
Righteousness	Good Works
Unrighteousness	Evil Works
Satan's People	Faith in Satan

Satan

The Narrow Path Leads To Eternal Life

Choices From The Heart

    God's people cannot be perfect; but they can surely try from a heart filled with God's Spirit. When they stumble and find themselves in a sinful situation, regardless of the cause, they immediately repent with specifics to a forgiving and loving God. They keep a short list of their sins with God.

"If we confess our sins, HE is faithful and just to forgive us our sins and to cleanse us from all unrighteousness." 1 John 1:9

"Cling tightly to your faith in Christ, and always keep your conscience clear. For some people have deliberately violated their consciences; as a result, their faith has been shipwrecked." 1 Tim. 1:19 NLT

GOD

God's People	Faith in God
God's Minimum Righteousness Standard	
Righteousness	Good Works
Unrighteousness	Evil Works
Satan's People	Faith in Satan

Satan

Non-Perfect Narrow Walk Pattern

Choices From The Heart

It can certainly feel like we go up and down in life. Every time we make a negative or sinful life choice, we move down towards Satan. Every time we make a positive or righteous choice, we move up towards God. The above illustration shows how we can walk a non-perfect narrow walk with God. First, we have to enter in by the narrow gate [Jesus Christ's spirit].

The narrow gate [Jesus] leads you into the narrow way [righteousness] and this is the realm of faith located above the minimum righteousness requirement [wherever that line is defined by God]. We might bob up and down a little. Every time we stumble and go negative, we repent with God immediately thereby keeping a very short list of sins with God. Immediate repentance also keeps our conscious clear.

In the preceding illustration, when we are very close to God, we are simply at the upper line [highest point] of the defined faith zone. Think of it as being constantly in God's presence and always making righteous choices from the heart. The minimum righteousness line can then be thought of as a point of being very aware of the world that we live in and somewhat distant from God's Holiness.

When we cross the minimum righteousness standard and move in a downward direction, we start to become friends with the world. The Bible teaches us that if we are friends with the world, we are at enmity with God. When we stay above the minimum righteousness line, we are Heaven bound and very righteousness aware. We are no longer spiritual babies that wander around in the wide path of destruction as was previously defined.

At all times there exists a "thought-life" that comes from our heart as Jesus indicated in Mark 7:20-23. Our thoughts are very important and God has provided further instructions to help guide our thought-life.

> **"And now, dear brothers and sisters, let me say one more thing as I close this letter. Fix your thoughts on what is true and honorable and right. Think about things that are pure and lovely and admirable. Think about things that are excellent and worthy of praise." Philip. 4:8 NLT**

Copyright 2005 Edward G. Palmer, All Rights Reserved.

Book of Edward—Chapter 7

Choices From The Heart

> # Your Thoughts Are A Choice From The Heart!

Yes, Norman was right when he taught us all to be positive thinkers. That is because he knew that our thoughts come from the heart.

You now understand that the TWO spiritual tools you will use in life are righteousness and sin. You understand that the TWO spiritual turfs you will operate on are God's and Satan's. And, you understand that you move in one direction or the other every time you make a choice from the heart. What does a backslider look like on this graphic illustration?

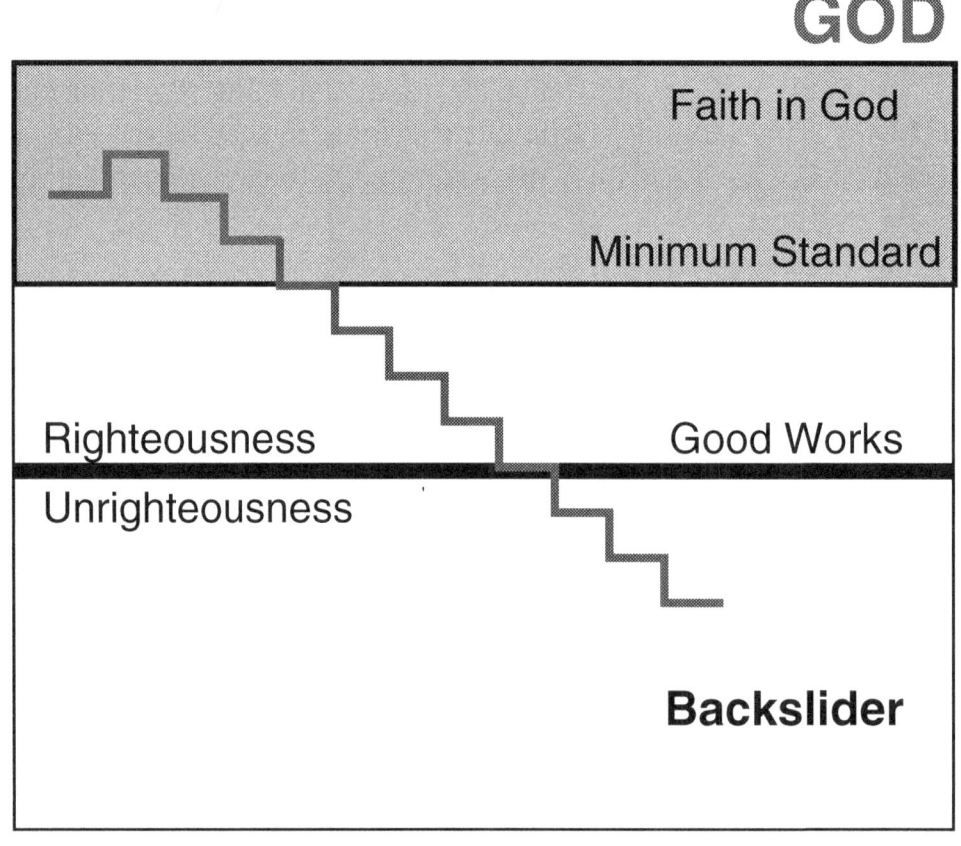

Backslider Pattern

Copyright 2005 Edward G. Palmer, All Rights Reserved.

Book of Edward—Chapter 7

Choices From The Heart

Of course, there are those people who give their hearts to God either with or without Jesus Christ and walk a righteous and narrow path with God the rest of their earthly lives. Such a walk might appear as a series of steps going straight up to God. However, it is also a narrow and straight line of righteous choices from the heart. It moves them from evil and sin and takes them directly into the arms of a loving and waiting God.

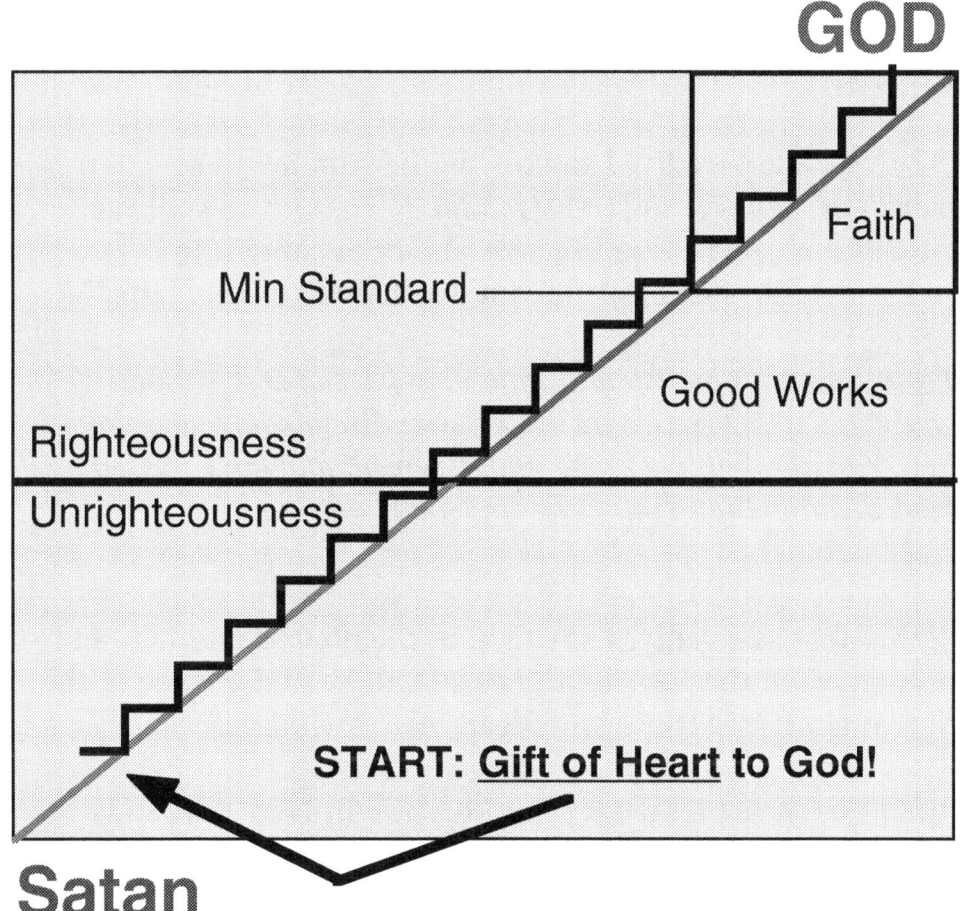

True Repentance Pattern

"Salvation belongs to our God who sits on the throne, and to the Lamb!" Rev. 7:10

Choices From The Heart

Please note that salvation is simply NOT just through Jesus Christ like Christian mythology teaches. Christianity has missed the message that God sent down with Jesus Christ. It will be explained in this book so keep on reading. Please note that in the above verse it is clear that salvation belongs to both God [who sits on the throne] and to the Lamb [Jesus Christ who is <u>not</u> sitting on the throne]. If this messes up Christian doctrine as taught by modern day Nicolaitans, you will have to make a choice from the heart to either believe God's Holy Word or to believe the Nicolaitans. Now consider the words of Jesus as the writer of Hebrews taught with some annotations.

> **"[24] Most assuredly, I say to you, he who hears my** *[Jesus]* **word and believes in HIM** *[God the FATHER]* **who sent me** *[Jesus]* **has everlasting life, and shall not come into judgment, but has passed from death into** *[eternal]* **life."**

Translation: If you listen to [and obey] Jesus and you believe in God the FATHER [who sent Jesus], you already have eternal life. You also will not come into judgment and have passed from death to life. Your belief in God is one out of righteousness.

> **"[25] Most assuredly, I say to you, the hour is coming, and now is, when the** *[spiritually]* **dead will hear the voice of the Son of God; and those who hear** *[obey]* **will live."**

> **"[26] For as the FATHER** *[God]* **has life in HIMSELF, so HE has granted** *[Jesus]* **the Son to have life in himself, [27] and has given him** *[Jesus]* **authority to execute judgment also, because he** *[Jesus]* **is the Son of Man." John 5:24-27**

Translation: Salvation or Life originates from God Almighty [the FATHER]. However, God has also given Jesus Christ eternal life to distribute. God has provided Christ with a power of attorney so that Christ may act on God's behalf. Do you get the picture that eternal life is in BOTH God [first] and Jesus Christ [second]?

Choices From The Heart

All of our choices for God do not carry the same weight or the same distance. The graphic below illustrates that some of our choices will carry us further towards God. Likewise poor choices from the heart can carry us away from God further and faster than one could suspect. Who or what controls the speed of your ascent or descent? Your heart and the thought-life that is inside of it control it all.

Can your speed be altered by who you are and what knowledge you have? Yes, it can. As we get closer to God, HIS expectations of our behavior increase. That is why God got mad at Moses for striking the rock and at David for counting his troops [war resources]. When you walk with God, HE expects you to trust in HIM and rely upon HIM. If you get as close to God as Moses and David did, you should know better than someone else that does not walk closely with God.

Clearly, each choice we make contains not only direction; but also distance and speed components. Clearly, your heart is in the driver's seat!

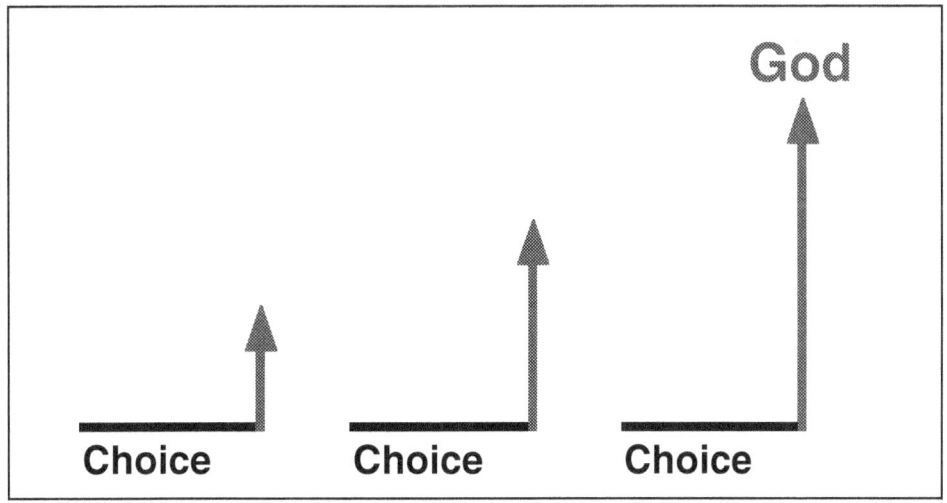

We CAN Make Bold Choices From The Heart

Choices From The Heart

Taking real conviction into play along with the components of great speed and distance from choices of the heart, a different righteousness pattern might emerge in some individuals. In the real conviction pattern shown below, the individual takes giant leaps for God and never looks back. They know how to get close to God and that is where they plan to stay. Such an individual is in the church of Philadelphia and will be raptured as explained by Christ. In the presence of God is where I want to live 24/7 all the days remaining in my life. Do you?

> "Because you have kept M%%Y%% command to persevere, I also will keep you from the hour of trial which shall come upon the whole world, to test those who dwell on the earth."
>
> Rev. 3:10

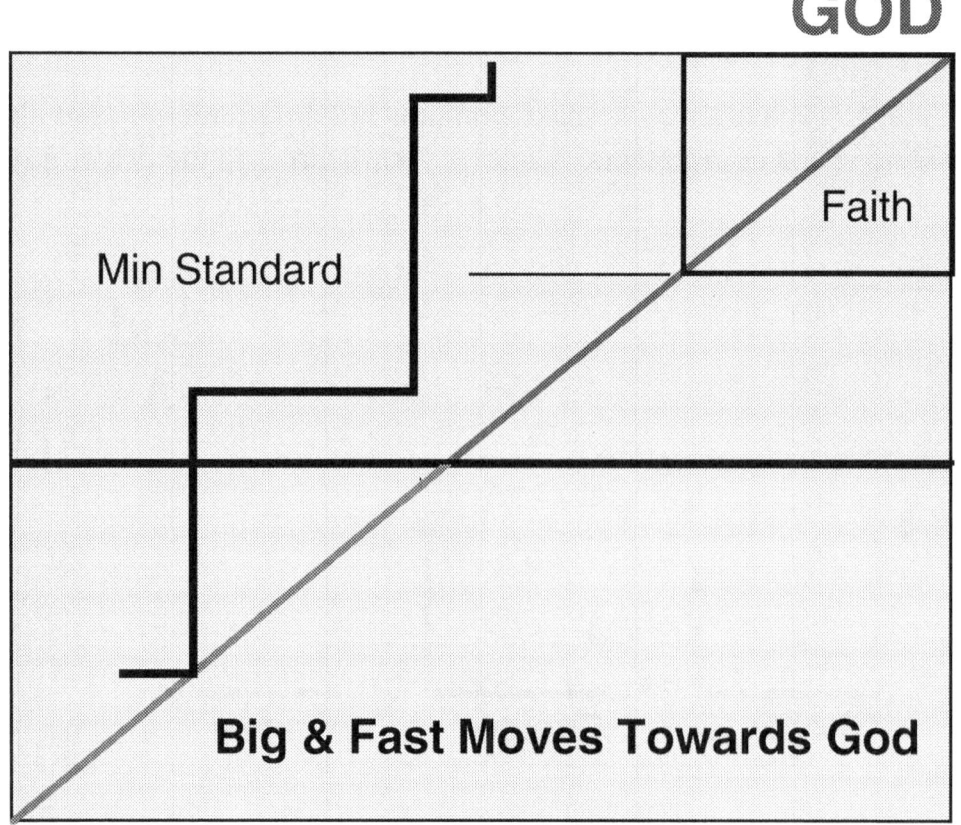

Real Conviction Pattern

Copyright 2005 Edward G. Palmer, All Rights Reserved.

Choices From The Heart

The opposite of a narrow and righteous walk with God is a walk in the wide path leading to destruction that Jesus talked about. Such a walk can be viewed as follows. It is a walk on both turfs and it is not a walk dedicated to God. You should understand that if you claim to belong to God, you have no business operating on Satan's turf [in darkness]. Consider these words.

"Do not be unequally yoked together with unbelievers. For what fellowship has righteousness with lawlessness? And what communion has light with darkness?" 2 Cor. 6:14

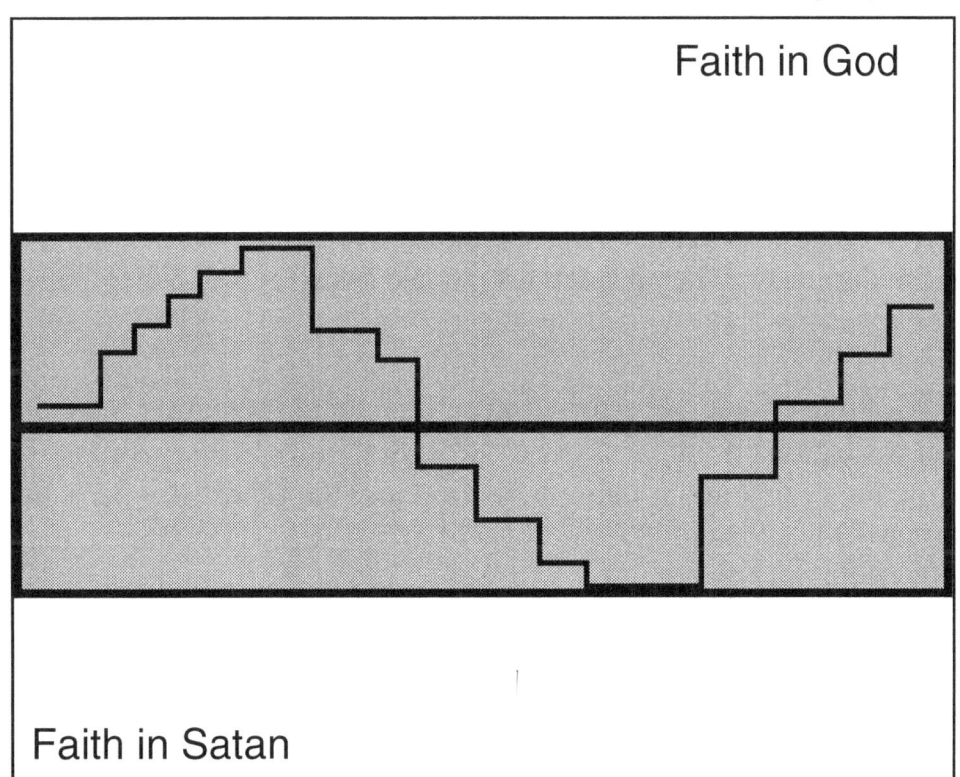

The Wide Path Leads To Destruction

Choices From The Heart

> **Then Jesus spoke to them again, saying, "I am the light of the world. He who follows me shall not walk in darkness, but have the light of life." John 8:12**

> **"I have come as a light into the world, that whoever believes in me should not abide in darkness." John 12:46**

God's Word is simple and clear that we, as children of the light [God], have no business fellowshipping with children of the darkness [Satan]. To do so represents a lack of sincerity [a sincere heart] with God. Those who walk the wide path leading to destruction operate with a mixture of righteous choices and unrighteous choices. They flip-flop through life believing they can have it both ways and they operate in the "world's view" of situational ethics [choices]. Whatever fits the current situation; that is what they do? These people are simply unsaved no matter how much they can mouth the words that Jesus is their Lord and savior.

Their actions speak very loud to a holy God and their life represents a walk in the darkness. They are lawless to use Jesus' words when he said: "I never knew you."

The above choice pattern is almost sinusoidal indicating those who walk this wide path could literally be 50/50 in their behavior. Fifty percent of the time they <u>think</u> about being with God and the other fifty percent of the time they are *actually* with Satan. Instead of situational dynamics, they need to practice righteousness dynamics. That would carry them upward in an ever-increasing way far away from sin. They lack an understanding that comes from a pure heart and are indeed double minded in their choices.

> **"Blessed are the pure in heart, for they shall see God."**
> **Matthew 5:8**

> **"Now the purpose of the commandment is love from a pure heart, from a good conscience, and from sincere faith"**
> **1 Tim. 1:5**

Choices From The Heart

> "Holding the mystery of the faith with a pure conscience."
> 1 Tim. 3:9

> "Flee also youthful lusts; but pursue righteousness, faith, love, peace with those who call on the LORD out of a pure heart." 2 Tim. 2:22

> "To the pure all things are pure, but to those who are defiled and unbelieving nothing is pure; but even their mind and conscience are defiled." Titus 1:15

Righteous Choices Come From A Pure Heart!

> "But let him ask in faith, with no doubting, for he who doubts is like a wave of the sea driven and tossed by the wind. For let not that man suppose that he will receive anything from the LORD; he is a double-minded man, unstable in all his ways." James 1:6-8

There is No Double-Mindedness In A Pure Heart!

Today, many Christians walk this wide path of destruction. They are double minded and have hearts that are not pure with God. If they had a heart that was pure with God, they would not consider sin. Instead, they would flee from sin knowing full well the impact it has on eternal life. These people think that as long as they are "sometimes" righteous, that is all they need. Their righteousness is like the scribes and Pharisees that Jesus talked about. They might do good works but they fall short of the minimum righteousness standard. It is Jesus who said: "For I say to you, that unless your righteousness exceeds the righteousness of the scribes and Pharisees, you will by no means enter the kingdom of Heaven." Matthew 5:20

Choices From The Heart

Have you made the choice to believe God and His Son Jesus yet? In other words, do you believe Jesus when he told you in clear and simple words that a minimum amount of righteousness *was required* to enter the kingdom of Heaven? Or, do you dismiss this teaching in favor of one from the pulpit of your pastor that is user-friendlier? Think about this, as your eternal life will depend upon your obedience to God and Christ. It does not depend upon your obedience to your pastor, church doctrine, family, friends, work associates or social club.

The graphic illustration I have used also conforms to a zone view if that would help illustrate God's Word. Consider the following four zones.

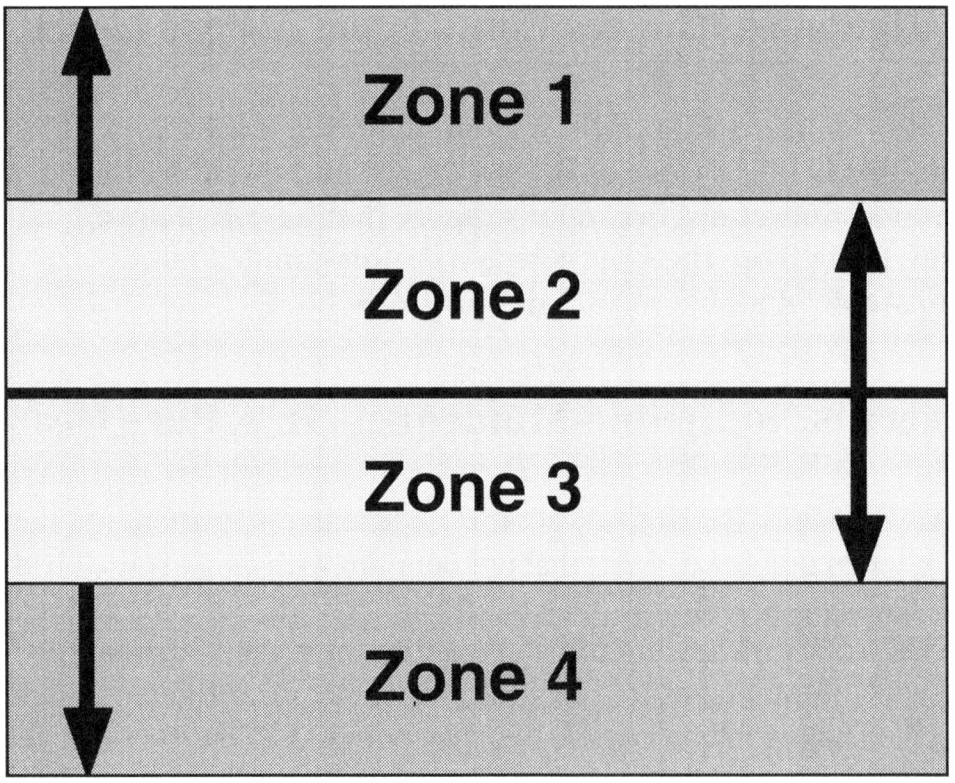

God & Satan's Turf Have Four Zones

Choices From The Heart

In the above illustration, God's turf is comprised of zones one and two. Satan's turf is comprised of zones three and four. In the middle is the line that separates righteousness from unrighteousness [sin], good from evil. Note the one-way arrows in zones one and four. These arrows represent the one-way nature of these zones and people who are committed to either God or Satan with their hearts. For those people, life's choices only point in a single direction, towards God or towards Satan.

Zones two and three represent the wide path that leads to destruction. These are the zones where people play around in life, spiritually speaking. They like to think of themselves as a good person albeit only to the extent that it is convenient in life and it fits in with their own assessment of the situational dynamics in play at any given choice. These are the people who do not stand on the truth and uphold righteousness at all costs. For them, grace means licentiousness and freedom from all moral boundaries. When life confronts them with an easy pass [sin], which no one will observe, they take it. This could be as simple as accepting extra change returned at the store. I.E. The clerk gives you change for a twenty, but you only gave him or her a five-dollar bill. After all, it was their mistake, wasn't it?

Think about those four zones above and the preceding illustrations and then consider the words contained in the book of Revelations chapter 3.

> **"I know all the things you do, that you are neither hot nor cold. I wish you were one or the other! But since you are like lukewarm water, I will spit you out of my mouth!"**
> **Rev. 3:15-16 NLT**

God knows those who belong to HIM and they operate inside of zone one only. These people are hot for God. God also knows who belongs to Satan and they operate in zone four. Those people are cold to God. The people who like to operate in zones two and three are lukewarm to God. They have never entered the one-way path that is above the minimum righteousness standard. That is why God says HE "will spit them out" [of Heaven]. That is why Jesus says: "I never knew you."

Choices From The Heart

Living In God's Zone Is A Choice From The Heart!

Zone one is where you experience the gift of God's Holy Spirit. It is the zone in which metaphysical events occur. It is the zone in which your reality is not always what you can see or observe with your own senses. When you are in zone one, your spiritual acumen observes a different kind of reality. It is a reality where God will manifest HIMSELF in the physical realm of this earth. It is the zone where miracles occur. It is a zone of faith.

When the writer of Hebrews wrote "it is impossible to renew them again unto repentance," he was referring to people who once entered zone one and then left the zone. They made a free will choice to no longer obey God. At one time, they were close to God but then left. They cannot return [repent again] according to Hebrews. The Bible is clear in Ezekiel that the "soul that sins shall die" and in Romans that the "wages of sin is death." Do you understand that sin can occur in any zone? Those who *practice* unrighteousness [sin] live in zones three and four or the wide path.

You've learned that there are two spiritual tools [forces] that are available in life. You've learned that there are two spiritual turfs that we operate on in life. You've learned that there are also two spiritual paths in life, a narrow path and a wide path. These teachings have been illustrated for you in graphic form so you can better understand God's Word. Beyond the spiritual tools, spiritual turfs and spiritual paths in life, God also teaches us that there are also only two types of people. There are godly and ungodly people. These two ways of life [living] are contrasted in Psalm 1:1-6.

Godly And Ungodly Contrasted!

"**Blessed is the man
Who walks not in the counsel of the ungodly,
Nor stands in the path of sinners,
Nor sits in the seat of the scornful;** [2]

**But his delight is in the law of the LORD,
And in HIS law he meditates day and night.** [3]

Copyright 2005 Edward G. Palmer, All Rights Reserved.

Book of Edward—Chapter 7

Choices From The Heart

> **He shall be like a tree**
> **Planted by the rivers of water,**
> **That brings forth its fruit in its season,**
> **Whose leaf also shall not wither;**
> **And whatever he does shall prosper. [4]**
>
> **The ungodly are not so,**
> **But are like the chaff which the wind drives away. [5]**
> **Therefore the ungodly shall not stand in the judgment,**
> **Nor sinners in the congregation of the righteous. [6]**
>
> **For the LORD knows the way of the righteous,**
> **But the way of the ungodly shall perish." Psalm 1:1-6**

God Knows Your Choices!

Modern Nicolaitans have really clouded up the idea of making a choice to be either godly or ungodly. They have also clouded up the idea of what is right and what is wrong. Nicolaitans would have you believe that there is a lot of gray matter [no purity of thought] in life. That is the reason why so many people live in zones two and three. They are content attending church on Sunday to ease their conscience. Society and its pulpits have not made God's Word clear to the people. You should know that this tactic is intentional. Satan is alive and well inside the church and a spiritual war wages for your soul.

Godly Or Ungodly Are Choices From The Heart!

It might seem unsophisticated to you to assert that there are two basic types of people in the world, godly or ungodly. However, this is not my opinion. I only point out what the word of God has to tell you. Only you can choose to believe and true belief is of the heart, backed by our behavior.

Believing The Bible Is A Choice From The Heart!

Choices From The Heart

There Are Two Spiritual:

- **Tools [righteousness & sin]**
- **Turfs [God & Satan's territory]**
- **Paths [narrow & wide]**
- **People [godly & ungodly]**
- **Choices [right & wrong]**
- **Directions [up & down]**
- **Destinations [Heaven & Hell]**

Your choices will determine the final destination of your soul. When you give God your heart, HIS Spirit will make its home inside you and help you to steadfastly make righteous choices. Your soul is going to end up in one of two places, either Heaven or Hell. Which choice will you make?

Now consider your choices when disaster strikes. If you buy into Christian mythology, you might think that nothing bad can happen to the true believer. There are many who teach a theology of health and wealth to God's people. If you suddenly find yourself sick, it must be because of your sin? If you are poor, it must be because you do not tithe? These topics will be discussed later in more depth. However, for now consider the misery that Job encountered when Satan launched his attack.

Job was a "man blameless and upright, and one who feared God and shunned evil [Job 1:1]." If you will recall the story you will note that the first disaster struck "when the Sabeans raided the oxen and donkeys" killing all the servants except the one telling the story. While the first servant was reporting another came saying "the fire of God fell from the Heaven and burned up the sheep and servants." Again, only this second servant escaped.

Copyright 2005 Edward G. Palmer, All Rights Reserved.

Book of Edward—Chapter 7

Choices From The Heart

While the <u>second</u> servant spoke, a <u>third</u> came and said: "the Chaldeans formed three bands, raided the camels and took them away, yes and killed the servants with the edge of the sword; and I alone have escaped to tell you." While the third servant spoke, a <u>fourth</u> came and said: "Your sons and daughters were eating and drinking wine in their oldest brother's house, and suddenly a great wind came from across the wilderness and struck the four corners of the house, and it fell ... and they are [all] dead."

In a matter of moments disaster struck Job and all that he had was lost including his sons and daughters. Job was barely able to take a breath before each succeeding disaster struck. Can you feel the pain in Job's chest? Yet, Job had faith in his God and responded with a choice from the heart.

"Naked I came from my mother's womb, and naked shall I return there. The LORD gave, and the LORD has taken away; blessed be the name of the LORD." Job 1:21

[22] "In all this Job did not sin nor charge God with wrong."

Job had a heart for God, in good times and in bad times. When disaster strikes you, what will be the choices from your heart? Will you turn away from God or have you learned to lean upon HIS higher understanding of our life? Has your soul fully understood that we will be alive in eternity a lot longer than in this physical body on earth? Will you <u>NOW</u> blame God? That was the strategy of Satan when it came to Job. To make him blame and curse God. It did not work.

I thought of Job this week as I got my own taste of such disaster. Just four days ago, my wife and I learned that she has inoperable cancer of the pancreas, spleen and liver. She has been told that in the worse case scenario she may only have ten days to live. In the best scenario she may have a few months up to a year. This woman is my childhood sweetheart and in a few months we will have been married 39 years. How do you say good-bye to someone you have loved for 43 years? Of course, she is at peace with God. The kind of peace that passeth all earthly understanding.

Copyright 2005 Edward G. Palmer, All Rights Reserved.

Book of Edward—Chapter 7

Myself? I didn't do so well on Wednesday night after the news. For 25 years I have been fearless with my own willingness to leave this planet and go home to God. Yet, it now seems my worse earthly fear materialized. I was being told that I would lose my dear wife Jackie. Quite frankly, I told God that I didn't know if I really wanted to continue living by myself. That reality was the toughest on me. There was so much physical pain that my wife asked me three times if she should call an ambulance. She thought I might be having a heart attack. I wasn't; it felt like the smashing of my heart into tiny little bits and pieces. I will never forget the physical pain I felt, which did not relent for two days. The emotional pain? It is not over yet.

Some Christians think that you can just exert spiritual power over the cancer that invades my wife's body. Just speak the word and she will be healed instantly. That is what I hear. You might add: "After all, you are an apostle, aren't you?" Healing is not simply a matter of demanding what you want from God Almighty. I will write a complete chapter dedicated to the issue of healing including at least two examples of where I did lay hands on people and they were saved from death. So what about Jackie? You'll have to wait to see what God has in HIS plan. For me, I have been reminded once again that no matter what life dishes out, I will praise the LORD. Simply put, till the day I leave this earthly existence, I will make choices from the heart that move me and those whom I love closer to the God that I love.

"Remain faithful even when facing death, and I will give you the crown of life." Revelations 2:10 NLT

"When you really walk with God, your choices will bring you closer to HIM, regardless of the earthly pain you may suffer." The Apostle Edward

It All Started When You Gave God Your Heart! Now, You've Decided To Make Righteous ...

Choices From The Heart

Book of Edward

Volume I
Notes & Bibliography

<u>Bible Translation Notice</u>: Permissions have not been sought to quote from the following Bible translations and the use of all copyrighted citations in this book are considered fair use under the United States copyright laws, which govern the publication of scholarly works. As already noted in the "Forward," a capitalization protocol has been introduced into many cited texts that make a clear distinction between God Almighty [Yahweh] and HIS only begotten human Son, Jesus Christ [Yashua]. Therefore, the cited text may not conform precisely to the printed text used herein in regards to any capitalized characters. Also, some verses are only partially presented for the sake of brevity in this book. The reader is therefore encouraged to examine all Bible citations while reading their own Holy Bible for a more complete and fuller understanding of God's Holy Word.

Forward (piii)

1 — (1611) *The Authorized King James Version* (KJV). <u>Comment</u>: The KJV is in the public domain in the United States and is therefore freely used and quoted by many people. Also, anyone can freely publish the KJV Bible.

2 — (1982) *Holy Bible, New King James Version* (NKJV). Nashville, Tennessee: Thomas Nelson, Inc. Copyright © 1979, 1980, 1982. <u>Comment</u>: The NKJV is an update to the KJV and closely parallels the KJV text. In the author's opinion, the NKJV Bible is an excellent way to enjoy the KJV without getting entangled in trying to comprehend its archaic and outdated English. See chapter 6 for a discussion of the errors found in the KJV.

3 — (1987) *The Amplified Bible* (AMP). La Habra, California: The Zondervan Corporation and the Lockman Foundation.

Notes & Bibliography - Volume I

4 — (1901) *American Standard Bible* (ASB).

5 — (1970) *New American Standard Bible* (NASB). New York, NY: Catholic Book Publishing Company. Copyright by the Confraternity of Christian Doctrine, Washington DC.

6 — Darby, John Nelson. Public Domain, 1833. *Darby Bible* (DB).

7— (1917) *Book of Enoch* (ENO). Richard Laurence 1883 Edition.

8 — (1978) *Good News Bible* (GN). Copyright by American Bible Society. New York: Thomas Nelson Publishers. Aka *"The Bible in Today's English Version;"* or, *"Today's English Version."*

9 — (1978) *Good News Bible; with Deuterocanonicals/Apocrypha* (GNB). Copyright by American Bible Society. New York: Thomas Nelson Publishers. Aka *"The Bible in Today's English Version; with Apocrypha."*

10 — (1995) *God's Word* (GW). Copyright by the Nations Bible Society. Database © 1997 by NavPress Software at www.WORDsearchBible.com.

11 — Mamre, Mechon (2002) *The Hebrew Bible in English according to the JPS 1917 Edition; HTML Version* (HEB). Internet: Http:www.mechon-mamre.org.

12 — Berlin, Adele and Brettler, March Zvi (Editors) (2004) *Jewish Study Bible* (JSB). Jewish Publication Society, TANAKH Translation. Oxford, New York: Oxford University Press.

13 — (1971) *The Living Bible* (LIV). Wheaton, Illinois: Tyndale House Publishers.

14 — (1996) *Holy Bible, New Living Translation* (NLT). Wheaton, Illinois: Tyndale House Publishers.

15 — (1988) *Microbible* (MB). Copyright by Ellis Enterprises, Inc.

Notes & Bibliography - Volume I

16 — (1988) *Morris Literal Translation* (MLT). Copyright by Ellis Enterprises, Inc., Oklahoma City, OK. See "The Bible Library" software.

17 — Moffatt, James A. R. (1922, 1924, 1925, 1926, 1935, 1950, 1952 and 1954). *The Bible: James Moffatt Translation* (MOF). Final Edition used and Copyrighted in 1994 by Kregel Publications, Grand Rapids, Michigan.

18 — (1984) *The Holy Bible, New International Version* (NIV). Copyright by International Bible Society. Published by Zondervan Bible Publishers.

19 — (1991) *The Holy Bible, New Century Version* (NCV). Aka *"The Everyday Bible."* Dallas, Texas: Word Publishing. Comment: Excellent modern English translation.

20 — (1985) *The New Jerusalem Bible* (NJB). Copyright by Darton, Longman & Todd Ltd and Doubleday, a division of Bantam Doubleday Dell Publishing.

21 — (1989) *The Revised English Bible* (REB). Copyright by Oxford University Press and Cambridge University Press. Comment: The Revised English Bible is a revision of The New English Bible.

22 — (1952) *Revised Standard Version* (RSV). Copyright by Division of Christian Education of the National Council of Churches of Christ in the United States of America. Zondervan Publishing House.

23 — (1989) *New Revised Standard Version* (NRSV). Copyright by Division of Christian Education of the National Council of Churches of Christ in the United States of America. Zondervan Publishing House.

24 — (1981) *Simple English Translation, New Testament* (SET). Copyright by International Bible Translators, Inc.

25 — Scherman, Nosson and Zlotowitz, Meir (General Editors). (1996) *The Stone Edition, Tanach* (TAN). Brooklyn, New York: Mesorah Publications, Ltd.

Notes & Bibliography - Volume I

26 — (1988) *Transliterated Bible* (TB). Copyright by Ellis Enterprises, Inc.

27 — Webster, Noah. Public Domain, 1833. *Webster's Bible* (WEB).

28 — Clarke, J. Public Domain, 1909. *Weymouth's New Testament* (WEY).

29 — Young, Robert. Public Domain, 1898. *Young's Literal Translation* (YLT).

Chapter 1

1 — (p10) Media and News reports of the 2000 Federal Elections in the United States indicated a near 50/50 split among voters who would call themselves Christian and that an estimated 90% of the black constituency voted for the Democratic Party presidential candidate.

Chapter 2

1 — (p23) Erwin W. Lutzer's book is an excellent read and explains why you can trust the Holy Bible from a historical translation perspective. Lutzer, however, recommends that you start reading your Bible at John 1:1. This I would take exception to, since it renders confusion over the identity of Jesus Christ from the start. Instead, I recommend you start reading in the Gospels at Matthew 1:1 and then read every red-lettered verse throughout the New Testament. Reading these words of Jesus Christ will bring you clarity, as Jesus never said that he was God. The red-letter verses stand as good theology in and of themselves and only the "Alpha and Omega" verse in Revelations is mis-interpreted as a statement from Jesus. See chapter 10 for a complete study of the phrase "Alpha and Omega" and why that phrase refers to God Almighty not Jesus.

Chapter 3

1 — (p37) Morris, William (1982) *The American Heritage Dictionary: Second College Edition.* Boston, Massachusetts: Houghton Miffin Company.

2 — (p57) Wilkinson, B. (2000). *The PRAYER of JABEZ.* Sisters, Oregon: Multnomah Publishers.

Notes & Bibliography - Volume I

Chapter 4
None

Chapter 5
None

Chapter 6

1 — (p121) Bryant, T & Et Al (1982) *Today's Dictionary of the Bible.* Carmel, New York: Guideposts.

2 — (p122) Ibid. *The American Heritage Dictionary.*

3 — (p122) Strong, James (1990) *The New Strong'S Exhaustive Concordance Of The Bible.* Atlanta, Georgia: Thomas Nelson Publishers.

Chapter 7

1 — (p134) Ibid.

2 — (p134) Microsoft Word:mac 2001 (1999) *Encarta® World English Dictionary.* Santa Rosa, California: Bloomsbury Publishing Plc.

Appendix A
A Real Salvation Prayer

OPENING PRAYER: FATHER God, let everyone who utters this prayer of salvation unto YOU, with a sincere heart, immediately feel the presence of YOUR Holy Spirit and equip them with the internal strength of conviction to stand tall for YOUR righteousness at all costs and even unto their own human death. Verily I say unto YOU that this is YOUR expectation of their [my] sincere heart. The Apostle Edward

INSTRUCTIONS: Pray out loud and offer up to God Almighty outstretched arms and the following prayer, on your knees, in the privacy of your prayer closet [private room, alone], and with your sincere heart. Verily I say unto you that your soul will see eternal life in Heaven upon the death of your earthly body if your heart is sincere with God to the point that your behavior turns to righteousness. Mark down the time, date and place of this gift of your heart to God and feel free to share this moment of time when you made a commitment to walk in God's ways with HIS priorities over your life.

PRAY: Heavenly FATHER, the only ONE and True God. YOU, who are also the FATHER and the only ONE and True God of my brother Jesus Christ whom YOU sent down as a living human sacrifice for the sins of all the humans in this earthly realm and world, hear this prayer from my sincere heart. This prayer comes from within the bowels of my spirit-soul and I fully understand that this is a one-way decision of my heart.

A Real Salvation Prayer

FATHER, I believe in YOUR only human begotten Son Jesus Christ. I believe that YOU sent Christ down to this earth and that he became the human being Jesus Christ [Yashua] in the flesh just like the flesh I have. I believe he had bones like I do, flesh like I do and blood like I do. I believe that his body on the cross was no different than any other human body on the cross. I acknowledge Jesus Christ is the Son of God; he is not God.

FATHER, I believe that he only spoke what YOU told him to say and that he only did what YOU told him to do. I believe that he was the final and perfect blood sacrifice for the forgiveness of the sins of mankind. FATHER I believe that includes my sins.

LORD, I fully acknowledge that by accepting Jesus Christ as my personal savior and brother that I am inviting his perfect spirit into my life to share this earthly body with me. Along with his spirit, I understand that you will also give me YOUR Holy Spirit and that YOU also will dwell within me.

I believe that the end result of my sincere acceptance of this gift of YOUR Son is the Oneness that I will share with YOU and him. Christ has taught me that I might live in perfect Oneness, Peace and Joy with YOU and him. O LORD, this is truly the sincere desire of my heart. I no longer want to be spiritually alone.

Therefore, I accept the precious gift of YOUR Son Jesus Christ and I repent of my past sins and sincerely regret every thought, action, behavior or anything that was displeasing unto YOU. I understand that with the precious gift of YOUR Son, YOU expect me to live a righteousness life the rest of my days on this earth.

Such a life entails living up to YOUR expectations and obeying what YOU and YOUR Son taught us in Holy Scripture. LORD, I acknowledge that I cannot be perfect in and of myself. I realize that to be like Christ requires that I "practice" righteousness and that I avoid sin to the best of my ability. I acknowledge that to continue willfully to sin is a tacit rejection of the gift of Jesus.

A Real Salvation Prayer

I also acknowledge FATHER that there will be unintentional and unknown sins that will come in my life. I understand that YOU and Christ will cover those types of sin and function as a guide in my life to keep me on the narrow path to Heaven.

FATHER, I acknowledge that YOUR Son is not a free pass on sins like so many Christians believe. Therefore, when I realize I have sinned against YOU in any way, I promise to confess that sin immediately and to keep a short list of my missteps with YOU. I know YOU are faithful to forgive under such conditions, but I also realize that if any life is filled with such confessions that it will be a testimony of an insincere heart. I recognize YOUR instructions in Ezekiel 18 and that Jesus has not altered YOUR criteria for punishing sinners. Therefore, keep me under YOUR wings O God and give me a pure heart unto YOU.

Having said this FATHER, I pray that you will dwell within me and help me to be the man [or woman] that you want me to be. I ask all of this in the name of Jesus Christ whom I confess with my mouth that he came in the flesh as YOUR only begotten SON. I acknowledge with my heart that YOU expect righteousness, a new life with changed behavior; behavior that glorifies YOU.

FATHER, help me to be an instrument of YOUR will even as Christ was such an instrument. Let this day be the first day of the rest of my life and help me to put away all offensive behavior and sin, which YOU hate. In the name of YOUR only begotten and beloved human Son Jesus, I pray. AMEN

Date and Time of Prayer: _____

Place of Prayer: _____

I First Told To: _____

_____

Copyright 2005 Edward G. Palmer, All Rights Reserved.

JVED Publishing

18140 Zane Street NW #410
Elk River, Minnesota 55330

www.jvedpublishing.org

Special Acknowledgements

The Apostle Edward would like to thank Dean and Jackie Mattila along with Vernon Enstad for their spiritual and emotional support during his four plus years of writing. Without their godly personal support and input, this work for God may not have been possible. This book was a spiritual journey for all four of them. A special thanks is also due Brian Mechler for his proof reading assistance. Book updates and errata data will be posted online at http://www.edwardtheapostle.org. For people in countries where the book is not available in print form or for those who prefer, it may be read and searched free online in English via web browsers at this web site.

The Apostle Edward asks ...
Are You Ready?

When he returns for souls, will Christ find you going about God's business? Will he find your spiritual light shining? If not, why? Do you even know why Christ stated those two salvation requirements?

There is an exodus from established churches by Christians who have found out that many churches no longer teach God's truth. The trend is worldwide and was the subject of a recent newsletter I received. These Christians read the Bible and compared what their church taught. They found that the Church supported many evil things that God abhors. In the process, they have asked themselves some fundamental spiritual questions:

- Can we support abortion if God abhors the shedding of innocent blood?
- Can we support Gay rights if God says homosexuality is abominable?
- Can we support a political party that seeks to excise God from everyday life?
- Can we support world friendship when it makes us HIS enemy?

Christian mythology is rampant. The Book of Edward discusses the above and many other important issues that the Church is now confronted with. Will you personally obey God's Word and the teachings of Jesus? If not, you are not saved. This book can reawaken your spirit and save your soul. At the very least, it will educate your heart.

I can remember the first experience in which I felt betrayed and confused by a pulpit teaching that did not line up and match what the word of God actually said. The basic choice you have, as a Christian, is whether you will adhere to God's Word or to the man made doctrines of your social group, your church, its hierarchy or its denomination.

There lies the main issue of salvation. You'll have to decide on God's Word if you want eternal life for in the end analysis you will be held accountable to HIS Word. Christians are leaving the established church and finding small fellowships or home churches as described in the New Testament. God has opened their eyes to HIS truth and if you read and study the Scriptures in this book, HE will open your eyes.

If desired, you may write to me in care of JVED Publishing. May your soul find the true salvation contained in the teachings of Jesus Christ. The Apostle Edward

www.ingramcontent.com/pod-product-compliance
Lightning Source LLC
Chambersburg PA
CBHW082119230426

43671CB00015B/2747